COLLECTOR'S GUIDE TO
MOTION LAMPS

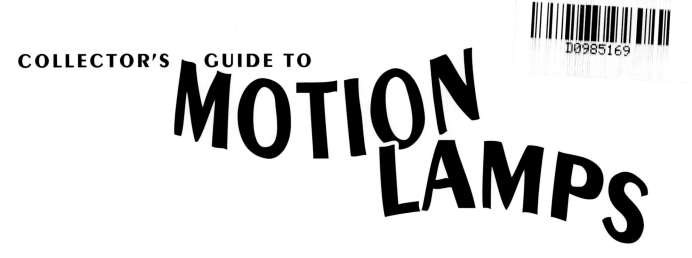

IDENTIFICATION
&
VALUES

With special sections on Advertising and Psychedelic Motion Lamps

Sam and Anna Samuelian

COLLECTOR BOOKS
A Division of Schroeder Publishing Co., Inc.

The current values in this book should be used only as a guide. They are not intended to set prices, which vary from one section of the country to another. Auction prices as well as dealer prices vary greatly and are affected by condition as well as demand. Neither the Authors nor the Publisher assumes responsibility for any losses that might be incurred as a result of consulting this guide.

Searching For A Publisher?

We are always looking for knowledgeable people considered to be experts within their fields. If you feel that there is a real need for a book on your collectible subject and have a large comprehensive collection, contact Collector Books.

Front cover: Forest Fire-Wildlife (1956) #2003; Train (1956) #763; Christmas Tree (1948 – 1952); Serenader (1931) #46; Waterski (1958) #771.

Back cover: Anna-Made-It Pink Flamingos (1994); Niagara Falls (1955) #76; Psychedelic Lamp; Budweiser (1970s); Totville Train (1948) B – 1.

Cover design by Beth Summers
Book design by Mary Ann Dorris

COLLECTOR BOOKS
P.O. Box 3009
Paducah, Kentucky 42002-3009

Copyright© 1998 by Sam and Anna Samuelian

Contents

❦ Dedication ❦

This book is dedicated to Mom and Dad Samuelian and Mom and Dad Arakelian. We owe you everything. You are the wind beneath our wings.

❦ Acknowledgments ❦

Our sincerest appreciation and thanks to the following special people:

Paul Miller, our dear friend. He has shared his fabulous lamp collection (second to none!) time and time again with anyone wanting to learn. He has generously supplied rare information and examples so that we could progress. He has found us lamps we could not find anywhere else, and has allowed us to borrow cherished pieces so that we could restore similar ones. Always ready to research and delve deeply into lamp trivia that probably no one else except he and your authors would care about, he has given of himself tirelessly. Mere thanks cannot suffice for the perseverance he showed when we photographed over 100 lamps in his collection. With ailing knees he went up and down the steps with us countless times to find and unplug lamps. When time progressed to two o'clock in the morning, and his eyes were literally closing down, he still cheerfully urged us to continue and finish our work. He is a person with the highest integrity and a model for others to emulate. A collector's collector, he is truly loved by all.

Linda and Bill Montgomery. Where would we all be without this lovely couple? They are true pioneers in the hobby, thanks to their book. They spent quite a few nights talking in lengthy phone calls to us as we tried to learn from their experience. They have provided photos of rare lamps in their collection, and have introduced us to many fine people with similar interests.

Gene Marcolina. He sold us a large portion of his extensive collection, which started us off in a big way. He was always friendly and enjoyed talking about lamps.

Catharine and Mahlon Fry. They traded with us on many occasions and allowed us to photograph some of their gems. Theirs is a collection to truly be enjoyed, as they display their lamps in small "island" areas in each room, creating a presentation which fits in so well with their decor and never seems overdone. Indeed a fine and loving couple who are always on the go, staying forever young. We will always remember the fly swatting session that followed the photographing of their lamps, since we had to leave the screen door to their farmhouse open to accommodate our power cord!

Fred Pribble. A gentleman and a scholar who shared photos of his collection of foreign lamps which he avidly sought out while living overseas. He has also provided us with a wealth of interesting background information and ideas for this book. His dedication and efforts are much appreciated.

Also, our warm thanks to the following collectors and dealers who have supplied photos, lamps, and encouragement in the task of completing this book: Bob Reed and Shari Haber, Jay and Joan Millman, Bob Nance, Jim and Kaye Whitaker, Larry Wesche, Arleen Strauss, John Clause, John Hershey, Lori and Dennis Trishman, Gerry Clemens, Ray Shope, Ray Strain, Rich Templin, Glenn Kennedy, John Forster, and especially Bill Holland, an author who convinced us to undertake this project and not be dissuaded by negatives. For invaluable tips on photography and quick processing of photos, we owe a debt of gratitude to Rob Eikler Photography and John Bogosian of the Camera Shops, Incorporated. Three cheers for Lisa Stroup, our very personable editor who guided us sharply while always giving us freedom of choice. And three more cheers for Collector Books. Every book dealer we spoke with gave them the highest praise, so it was easy to choose them as our publisher. We hope their foresight in deciding to print our book is rewarded enthusiastically.

Finally, to the many dealers and collectors we have patronized, we politely ask that you try not to raise prices after seeing this book!

❧ Foreword ❧

Motion Lamps Rub Me The Right Way
By Penny Marshall — Actress, director, TV and movie star, and a very avid collector

My name is Penny Marshall and I'm a motion lamp junkie.

The first motion lamp I ever owned had New York City's skyline and the Statue of Liberty on it. I bought it at a swap meet during the 1970s when I was living in Los Angeles, but still pining away for New York where I had grown up. Whenever I looked at the lamp, it made me think of New York and helped ease my homesickness. That's what I like best about motion lamps: I feel like I'm going somewhere, but I'm not leaving my living room. They move and you don't have to. If I sit on my sofa at home and watch television, they call me a couch potato. But if I sit on my sofa and watch one of my motion lamps, they say "Leave Penny alone. She's traveling."

I own more than 45 motion lamps and I keep them in my house in Los Angeles as well as my apartment in New York. Most motion lamps are not made of glass, which is great because when you live near a fault line anything made of glass eventually breaks in an earthquake anyway. The lamps are a perfect accessory for anyone living in California or anyone who may be a little klutzy like me. I do, however, own a few glass ones and those are in my New York earthquake-friendly apartment for safe keeping.

My collection started out kind of slowly, but as my compulsion for shopping picked up, so did my inventory of lamps. I'm sure you've heard about celebrities collecting things like vintage cars, yachts, diamonds, and even husbands, but I like to be a little different. I collect paperweights, tiny shoes, snow globes, hooked rugs, maps of the United States, trench art, and about a zillion other quirky things. But my collection of motion lamps has always been one of my favorites and most talked about. It's not the kind of collection you're gonna see in every house. Also, unlike normal lamps that look naked and ugly when you put

An Anna-Made-It lamp, created especially for Penny. The photo used for it was taken during the winter shoot of *The Preacher's Wife*. On the back, we have answered her request for a lamp with a big L on it.

5

them up in high places with a light bulb glaring at you, these lamps can be easily seen and look great whether they are placed low on a bookshelf, high on top of a cabinet or somewhere in between. I display them in my foyer, living room, and even in my grandson's playroom.

Motion lamps also look cute underneath wrapping paper and a bow. I've gotten them as presents and given them to friends on special occasions. I also used one as a prop when I directed *The Preacher's Wife*. We were on location in New York one day and were supposed to shoot outside, but the terribly bad weather made us change our schedule. So we quickly decided to move inside. However, the interior set wasn't ready. I sent the production designer over to my apartment and told him to grab whatever he wanted to dress up the set quickly. He came back with my choo-choo train motion lamp and suggested that we use it in the scene with Whitney Houston's little boy, played by actor Justin Pierre Edmund. The lamp was not only perfect for the scene, but Justin also fell in love with it. I ended up giving it to him to keep as a souvenir of the film. (Of course, I later bought myself another train lamp because I loved it too.)

My collection covers a range of subjects from animals (geese, gold fish, circus animals, ducks, butterflies) to romantic destinations (Niagara Falls, a warm fireplace, a snowstorm, a Japanese landscape, moonlight on a river) to modes of transportation (airplanes, trains, cars, boats, buses). Over the years I have discovered it has become harder and harder to find lamps to buy that weren't dented. Then I found Sam and Anna Samuelian. I first met them at the Triple Pier Expo collectibles show in New York several years ago, and I've been buying lamps from them ever since. They not only tell me when the good ones come in, they also restore my lamps when they occasionally wear down.

It's great that Sam and Anna have published a book about motion lamps because I can look through it and see which ones I want to add to my collection. If anyone comes across one with an "L" for Laverne on it, let me know (see lamp on page 5). The only downside to this book is that now everybody will know what a great hobby collecting motion lamps is, and I'll have more people to compete with for the good ones. Hopefully there are enough motion lamps to go around. If not, we can enjoy the wonderful pictures right here. I think Sam and Anna and motion lamps are in a league of their own.

Introduction

a note about motion sickness

Welcome to our book and the ranks of the happy society of collectors who have motion sickness. No, not the kind you get on a cruise ship that makes the stomach queasy to the point where you feel you are about to lose it. No, this is the collecting kind you get when you gaze on another available motion lamp and the stomach becomes increasingly queasy, because you know you are about to lose your money! One purchase usually leads to another and then another and, before you know it, you have a bad case of motion sickness.

But fear not. Help is here with each page you turn. If you are a beginner and have pre-motion sickness, we hope the insightful text and the irresistible photos will guide and educate. If you are an advanced case and have worn out the pioneer motion lamp book by Linda and Bill Montgomery, we hope to re-awaken your interest by exposure to countless "new" lamps, of which you (and often we) were unaware. Or you could simply be a carrier of motion sickness, a collectibles dealer. You may want only to infect others with motion sickness by using the book to identify and price items for sale. Well, you too are welcome, since we the motion sick need your assistance in finding these often elusive lamps. We ask just one small favor. When you stand holding a lamp before our slightly trembling motion sick bodies, please, please be fair with your pricing. You know if you are, we will be back for more!

A very real and genuine enthusiasm was felt by these authors during the countless hours spent putting together this book. There were moments during the year and a half of production when it seemed that just one more revision or one more photo retake would put us into an institution, but somehow we made it to the end. Surely the understanding that this was a labor of love helped see us through. If our efforts inspire, educate or excite you, then we feel our goal has been achieved.

We have paged through the Montgomery motion lamp book endlessly, reading and re-reading about each precious lamp we hoped to someday find. In fact, we handled that little book until it was all thumb worn. We will derive the greatest pleasure knowing that many of you will use our book with the same fervor!

This is motion sickness in full bloom.

❧ **Background** ❧

People are attracted to motion, and there is always fascination with things that move, whether they are wind-up toys or lamps that come to life when the switch is thrown. Our focus will be any electric lamp that provides motion due to the heat of a light bulb. Motion created by a motor is a study that we hope to tackle in another book.

Motion lamps have had many names. Looking through old advertisements will yield the following names: heat lamps, action lamps, radio lamps, TV lamps, rotating lamps, revolving lamps, scene-in-action lamps, spinner lamps, animated lamps, moving picture lamps, roto-action scenic lamps, and more. One collector we know simply calls them "lights!" Many early patent descriptions used the term animated lamps. This is a worthy term, but not all motion lamps are truly animated, as we will explain. We will use the term "motion lamp" as the most accurate means to describe this collectible.

Motion lamps first appeared in the teens of the twentieth century. Many were experimental and were never actually produced. By the early twenties, some oil burning motion lamps were on the market, and by the late twenties when electricity was entrenched in our everyday living, electric powered motion lamps became popular.

Some of the earliest motion lamps were radio lamps. Purchasers used them to grace the tops of radios, allowing listeners to gaze while hearing broadcasts. Years later, the lamps graced the tops of televisions to give the viewer something to look at when commercials became boring, or to provide entertainment when the TV was off, or even to ward off poor eyesight, which was rumored to be an effect of watching TV without some light source being on nearby.

Aladdinette Oil Lamp.

By the mid-fifties, these lamps finally had a purpose of their own. They were purchased to do what they do best — provide illumination and fascinating motion while quietly entertaining. They can be placed singly and distinctively stand out, they can be placed in creative groups by picture themes, they can be positioned on rows and rows of shelves, or hung on walls if they are wall mount styles. Any way they are displayed, they will surely command attention. As we said earlier, people are attracted to motion. We have found that to be a rule when working antique and collectibles shows. No matter what we are selling, motion lamps will bring people to our booth like magnets. Not everyone will buy, but all will admire and converse when under the spell of these small yet mighty devices.

We are always asked about the parts that make up a motion lamp. All motion lamps have an electrical cord and plug, a light bulb and socket, often an on-off switch, a base to support the shade, a metal rod with a sharp point at the top on which the cylinder or shade pivots, a cylinder, often an animation sleeve, and a scene which is animated or simply revolves.

a note about lamp styles

There are several basic styles of motion lamps. First and foremost are the *true animated lamps*. These have a lighted scene on the outer shade which appears to move with some form or action. Let us look inside this style lamp. A light bulb is usually in the center, and a pivot rod is mounted either above or next to the bulb. The rod is topped with a sharp point, and on this point a cylinder pivots on a tiny glass or jeweled metal cup. The top of the cylinder, called a fan, has paper or metal

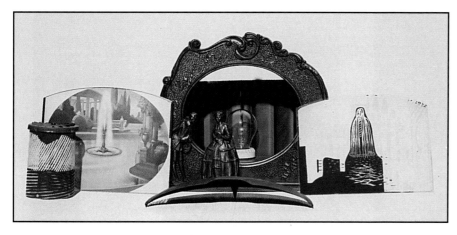

Parts of a typical 1930s lamp.

Parts of a typical 1950s lamp.

A true animated lamp.

fins that allow air to pass through. When the light bulb warms, the hot air rises and spins the cylinder in a clockwise or counter clockwise direction, depending on the angle of the fins. The body of the cylinder, usually plastic, will have patterns stenciled on it in white or various colors. The patterns produce shadows of light that pass through and fall onto the outer shade which has two sections. First, there is an inner sleeve usually made of plastic. We call it the animation sleeve. This sleeve, like the cylinder, has white or colored patterns stenciled on it. Second, the shade has an outer plastic or glass sleeve that has a scene lithographed on it (or a paper scene under glass, or a paper scene over glass, or both). The light that started with the bulb passes through the cylinder and the animation sleeve, then projects onto the outer scene sleeve, creating the illusion of motion. In areas where motion is not desired, stenciled patterns on the animation sleeve block the light projection. For example, a stream of water flowing in a lake should not flow through a nearby ship, so the image of the ship is blocked by a pattern on the animation sleeve. Incidentally, some of what we are calling sleeves are flat panels on lamps with a flat shape, like various 1930s metal and glass Scene-in-Action lamps.

The color of the cylinder or animation sleeve can be quite important. The tone of the color used will enhance or affect the graphic image on a lamp. The wonderful Scene-in-Action Forest Fire is very realistic because a yellow cylinder passes colored light through a red animation sleeve. Red and yellow flames, the natural colors of fire, are the resulting image projected onto the similarly colored scene graphic. The fine Goodman Lighthouse includes a multi-colored cylinder for its earliest production models that produces a lovely background of changing colors against the lighthouse. Later models were supplied with a single color cylinder that projected the same fine animation but were lacking the added appeal of a rainbow background. Interestingly enough, Econolite seldom used color in their cylinders. With the exception of colored trees and houses for certain transportation theme lamps, and dark gray colored snow scene cylinders, most of their production cylinders were drawn in white. They did, however, use color in making their animation sleeves. It is possible that the rich colors employed in creating their scenes needed little enhancement via cylinder or animation sleeve coloring. And while we are comparing cylinders, why not point out differences in construction? Scene-in-Action, Econolite, and others used a diagonal cut in making their cylinders and carefully joined the edges along the diagonal line. Goodman, Rev-o-lite, and others used a simpler vertical cut and joined the edges at the seam. Diagonal cuts, when precisely joined, are superior in that no extraneous shadows or blips will be seen by the eye as the seam passes by. Vertical cuts are sometimes more visible since the entire seam from top to bottom hits the line of projection in one spot.

True animated motion lamps are the most prevalent, most popular, most intricate, and certainly the most impressive. If the operation of a true animated lamp described earlier confused our readers, we hope the *limited animation rotating shade lamp* will be easier to understand. It differs in that the cylinder is stationary.

8

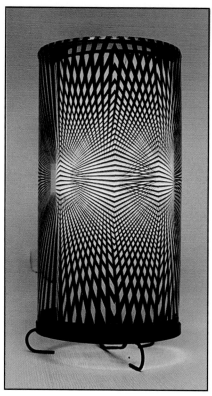

Two types of limited animation lamps.

A distortion animation lamp.

The cylinder still has patterns stenciled on it, but it does not move. What moves is the outer shade, pivoting on the metal rod. The outer shade in this style has only one sleeve, the scene sleeve, and light effects appear on it as it revolves. Liquor companies have used this simpler type to attract the attention of their customers. Often just glistening words or images appear, but the effect is ten times more interesting than static images. These limited animation lamps are also popular, can be captivating, and are fairly prevalent. Another style of limited animation lamps uses a stationary outer shade with a rotating cylinder. Again, there is no animation sleeve. Most psychedelic lamps employ this construction, as do many advertising lamps. They can be equally or more effective than their stationary cylinder, rotating shade cousins. Quality of design will separate the mediocre from the superior, as it will in almost any lamp.

Still another type of motion lamp is the *distortion animated lamp*. Its effects are derived from a pleated layer of plastic or glass on the shade that bends and distorts the images projecting from the cylinders. Goodman used this style more often than any other company and it served them well and kept costs low. Even though a simpler form of animation, colors, and motion can be quite pleasing with this style, as a good butterflies or fish lamp will prove.

The simplest type we have saved for last, especially for readers who just like to see something spin around. The *non-animated revolving shade lamp* has a shade with a scene printed on it that rotates either left or right. A lamp of pin-up girls drawn by Gil Elvgren and produced by Econolite is a stunning example of this style. The images are attractive and can be seen easily as the shade moves. These are often children's lamps and may include an inner scene around which the shade revolves. They may be fragile due to lightweight construction, are hard to find in good condition, and range from dull to delightful.

A non-animated revolving shade lamp.

While minor variations of all the above styles can be seen, you are now aware of the basic types of motion lamps waiting to be found and collected. The ones that appeal to you will be best determined by seeing and experiencing them. You may want to purchase all types and have a well-rounded collection, or you may want to specialize and limit purchases to the types that satisfy you most. Our 77-year-old friend Catharine Fry buys lamps using a very fitting criterion: they must "turn her on!" Whatever your choices, the bewitching effects they create will surely please and amuse.

Themes displayed on motion lamps produced from the earliest times to the present are interesting and varied. Without a doubt, the most frequently occurring theme is flowing water, followed in frequency by burning fire. The most abundant of the flowing water lamps are the Niagara Falls lamps. Widely popular when released, and still desired today, countless of these were produced. Of the burning fire types, forest fires lamps were far and away the most often manufactured. Fish, butterfly, and duck themes were used frequently and appeared in many different formats. Transportation themes covered automobiles, trains, sailing ships, steamboats, trucks and buses, airplanes, and more. Trains seem to have sold the best originally, followed by ships and automobiles. Trucks, buses and airplanes are seen much less frequently. Some themes are only seen on one or two lamps. The Scene-in-Action 1933 Chicago World's Fair lamp is the only lamp ever produced that features fireworks which shoot in the air in colors, and then dissipate. Moreover, some themes lend themselves to animation more readily than others. Fire effects, even when done poorly, still look convincing on most lamps. But an object waving in the wind is much more difficult to convey, even in the hands of a skilled artist. Overall, the variety of themes found is copious enough to please collectors, yet there are many unexplored themes which could add greatly to our choices. Motorcycles, super heroes, and wind surfers represent just a few thematic examples that could enrich future motion lamp collections. With imagination, skill, and enthusiasm, we will hopefully see new themes appear!

a note about nomenclature

Wherever possible, we have used names and model numbers assigned to lamps by checking original advertisements, original literature, or original boxes. Often names are printed right on the lamp, making identification simple. However, when this information was not available, we assigned a descriptive name to each lamp, using quotation marks around our wording. Names that appear in *Animated Motion Lamps* by Bill and Linda Montgomery (L-W Books, out of print) have been used here as correct names unless errors have been discovered. It is hard to re-learn a name you have used for years. For instance, the Montgomery book calls Econolite #774, "Airplanes," a perfectly good descriptive name. But we discovered on an original name tag that Econolite actually named it "Jets." We may try calling a lamp by its proper name, but the name we have used for years keeps getting in the way! The Goodman lamp known as "Mountain Waterfall" would have been more appropriately called "Yosemite Falls," since there is little doubt that the scene is derived from the famous landmark. Ironically the factory name for this lamp is worse than either of the above, as it was called simply "Waterfall-Campfire". On the other hand, the Econolite lamp known as "Oriental Scene" was actually called "Oriental Garden" when it was released, as a recent mint in the box example proved. We welcome any reader insight into assigning more accurate names in the future.

a note about production dates

While many lamps are clearly dated, many more are not. Thus it has been a challenge to assign a release date to the lamps presented here. When we are fairly certain of accurate dates, we have listed them after the names of the lamps. When we have used our judgment and comparisons to other lamps, a question mark follows the date. But we want to stress here that dating is relative. For instance, most Scene-in-Action lamps are clearly stamped with a 1931 date, but we know that the company produced lamps from 1926 through 1936. Similarly, the Goodman Lighthouse lamp is dated 1956, but it was probably produced from that time right through 1971 since we have found examples from that late date and have seen model variations on this and many other lamps released in different time periods. On the other hand, lamps like the Econolite 1962 Seattle World's Fair were probably made for just one year. Generally, lamps with later release dates will be harder to find, since they were produced for shorter time periods and in lesser numbers.

a note about our photos

Throughout this book, we have tried to photograph each lamp using the best examples we could find. In cases where a rare lamp existed only in fair condition, we have photographed it rather than leave it out, so the reader can at least have some type of photo to view. We have also tried to provide additional photos to illustrate and strengthen the text. Photographing one-sided lamps was straightforward, but when it came to photographing lamps with two or more sides, some decisions had to be made due to space considerations. Therefore, with multiple-sided lamps only one photo was taken of the primary or "A" side if the scene on the secondary side was an extension or continuation of the same graphic (Niagara Falls lamps are a good example). However, if the secondary side featured an entirely different graphic (like many car or train lamps), both sides were photographed. If additional detail or close-up shots were needed, they were also included. In cases where round and oval lamps of the same scene were released, we have photographed both types randomly since it is difficult to discriminate a round model from an oval in photos (a little known fact is that the photos in the Montgomery book usually show one side of a lamp in round format and the other side of the same lamp in the oval format). Whenever possible, we tried to capture lamps that were lit so that the animation would be visible. Some lamps photograph better unlit, so we occasionally captured them turned off. Overall, the animation detail is extremely difficult to capture on film, so keep in mind that a lamp in person will usually look much more vivid. We have fully described the animation of each lamp to amplify characteristics the photos may lack. Finally, capturing the color and detail in pleated shade lamps was also quite difficult and not always satisfactory.

❧ **Values and Availability** ❧

We have been actively buying, selling, and collecting motion lamps full time for seven years now. During this period we have witnessed prices double and triple, making it difficult to find bargains anymore. About a year ago we were speaking to a collector at a large collectibles show. As he admired our display of about 50 lamps, he remarked that two years before he had purchased some of the same lamps currently priced at $125.00 for only $50.00. Both my wife and I scoffed at this, saying he had to be mistaken. Upon arriving home and checking our books, we were dumb founded—he was absolutely right. We had sold him lamps for $50.00! Presently, we are probably paying as much as $125.00 to put the same lamps in our inventory.

We have come to realize that one-third to one-half of the lamps we find need work. Work takes time and time is money, so when buying a lamp to sell to a dealer, keep in mind that he must buy a good clean lamp at about half the market price to make an average living. By this we mean a living in which a dealer can pay his bills, buy more stock, and have money left for everyday life. If a lamp needs work, he must buy it for about one-third of the market price or less. The average collector usually has a hard time accepting this, but we refer you to the well-thought-out articles that collectibles expert Harry Rinker has written on this subject and published in national collectibles publications. He has repeatedly asserted that, with collectibles in a relatively low price range (like motion lamps that typically sell from $100.00 to $400.00), a dealer must at least double his money to make a minimal living. Add to the cost of the lamp a dealer's restoration, advertising, showcase rental, electricity, and storage, not to mention the large chunk Uncle Sam takes out of his pocket. Keep these factors in mind when selling to a dealer and you'll see what frustration they face when people want to sell lamps to them for full retail. And we can't stress enough the importance of having a

price in mind when offering a lamp for sale. The world of specialized collectibles is often a small world, so asking for an offer can pit friends against each other in bidding wars. This creates trouble and hard feelings and can even backfire on the person asking for offers. No one wants to make free appraisals, especially when the appraisals are used against them to jack up a price. Have a fair price in mind ahead of time, or ask friends about value and then call one person at a time with your price. Ultimately, everyone will be happier this way!

Prices in this book are based on actual sales realized and never wildly varying auction figures. Prices are also based on conference with other lamp dealers, and educated guesses in the care of extremely rare, seldom seen pieces. Prices seem highest on the West Coast, catching up on the East Coast, and somewhat lower in middle America. As with any collectible, condition is most important, while rarity and desirability are also important factors. Prices listed after each lamp description are for lamps in excellent to mint condition. Prices must be adjusted down accordingly for any lesser condition. If a mint condition lamp is valued, for instance, at $250.00, an excellent example may be only $200.00, while a good example may be about $150.00, and a fair example around $100.00; a poor example may be as low as $50.00 or even less. The wide range of price between the mint example at $250.00 and the poor one at $50.00 should well illustrate the point we are trying to make about condition. All too often, people will misuse price guides by valuing their pieces at top levels without considering the condition of what they have. The factors of rarity and desirability may easily influence the level of condition you would be willing to accept, as often the "I might never see it again" feeling overcomes your hesitation to purchase. Overall, buy with your eyes open and buy only that which adequately satisfies your requirements. But remember never to underestimate the added value a lamp will have when it has been restored as close as possible to factory-new standards. A new and proper bulb, a new and safe line cord and plug, a cleaned and polished pivot point, jewel cup and base, important cosmetic improvements, and of course all the correct parts, will always enhance value.

People ask where we find our stock, since they feel lamps are difficult to locate. Lamps are quite difficult to locate. They were originally sold mostly in industrial areas and in low-cost stores. That is why Pennsylvania, among other states, has been such a good source for lamps. In some states (Texas is a good example) they are practically non-existent. Being a very specialized collectible, you might go to a hundred garage sales and not come home with even one lamp. Flea markets are somewhat more likely to yield finds, since more people have dug them out of houses as values have increased. High level antiques stores are only now starting to accept them as valid merchandise. The best sources have been antiques and collectibles malls and shows. Most of our business is mail order, a great way to find what you want with no travel and little searching. Advertising for wants may also be an effective way to find what you are looking for. Also check the Internet for advertisements and auctions, because online sales are increasing by leaps and bounds.

The now out-of-print Montgomery book provided the foundation for the hobby of collecting motion lamps and gave it added credence. Even when that book first appeared in 1991, most dealers wanted one-and-a-half to two times the listed prices. In fact, most seemed to feel the listed prices were close to wholesale. This is not the case today, as prices have risen rapidly and have somewhat stabilized. We caution dealers and collectors alike with a warning. Do not assume prices herein are low or outdated and immediately increase asking prices since your lamps "must be worth more." We have seen good markets falter with uncalled for price increases that are simply too high for these markets to bear. We have been, and currently are, right on the cutting edge of the motion lamp field and are in a good position to give this advice. Please take a conservative approach and the market will hopefully grow in a slow and healthy manner instead of becoming a shooting star that soon loses its light.

Our hope is that this new book will greatly expand the foundation laid by the first book with the large number of lamps included and the attention to detail we have tried to maintain. We truly love our collection of lamps and strongly hope our enthusiasm is felt throughout each page. When all is said and done, motion sickness is a great thing to have and live with — so spread the word and let those lamps shine!

a note about original boxes

While having an original box in fine condition can double the value of toys and other collectibles, the value of a box to a motion lamp collector is minimal. This is largely due to lamps having usually been packaged in ordinary cardboard boxes with little printed information. Finding a lamp in an original box does have one bonus — the lamp inside can be in exceptional condition. Also, it is possible that some related printed information may be included. Overall, a lamp's value will only be increased about five to ten percent with an original box in fine condition at this time. We encourage collectors to keep boxes regardless, since relatively few have survived. The only boxes surviving in any quantity are those that held Econolite Christmas tree lamps. These are still around because they were often used to store the lamps from season to season. Of course, exceptional boxes with color graphics will be more valuable than plain ones. In the long run, we have seen only one Scene-in-Action box and a few Goodman boxes, and only one or two from any other smaller companies. Econolite boxes seem to be the most easily found.

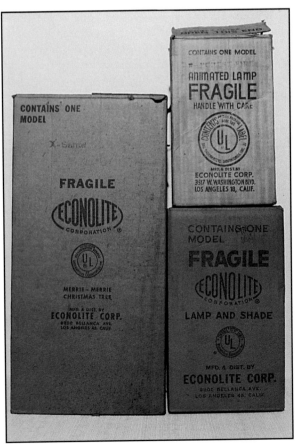

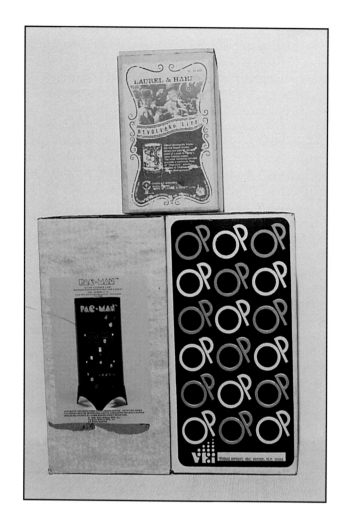

a note about parts for lamps

If a part is needed for any purpose, it has value to the needy person. Otherwise, a part can be useless junk. We suggest that you pay within reason, based on your degree of need. Bases or tops may be worth five to twenty-five dollars. A cylinder may be worth twenty-five to fifty dollars to complete a good lamp. Animation glasses or sleeves may be worth fifty to seventy-five dollars.

Using an original part is far easier than trying to recreate one and will never devalue a piece. Also, keep parts around that you may need in the future. Just try finding a red plastic top for a Hopalong Cassidy lamp when you must have one! Cylinders and tops are the most often needed parts, so never discard these. Sometimes a lamp purchased for parts will become a better lamp than one you already had with a little exchanging of parts.

❧ Scene-in-Action Corporation ❧

Starting with the Scene-in-Action Corporation is a must since they were one of the earliest producers of motion lamps. The key man here was Albert Sabath, who designed most of their product. The company was in business from 1925 through 1936. Its first location was at 110 Dearborn St., Chicago, Illinois. In 1927 the corporation moved to 1603 South Michigan, and in 1928 it moved a couple of blocks away to 1809 Indiana Ave., where it stayed until 1936. Albert Sabath became president of the company in 1929 and remained in this position until 1935. In 1935 the company changed its name to the Scene-in-Action Advertising Corporation and moved its corporate offices to 400 West Madison St. but probably retained its manufacturing plant at the old address, as the company secretary listed 1809 Indiana as his address. In 1936 the company failed to file as a domestic Illinois corporation and there is no listing of a filing for any succeeding years. In 1935, however, the Rev-o-lite Corporation from New Brunswick, New Jersey, filed for the first time as a foreign corporation doing business in Illinois. This first filing coincides with the year Scene-in-Action finally became defunct as a corporation. Judging by the construction and similarity of some Rev-o-lite lamps to Scene-in-Action models, we feel that Rev-o-lite took over the remaining inventory of Scene-in-Action and released lamps featuring Scene-in-Action graphics and inner parts in Rev-o-lite frameworks.

Producing lamps involved engineers who would take the art work designed for the scenes and then work to devise and construct the animation glasses and associated cylinders, many of which had to be carefully aligned for the finished product. Scene-in-Action used durable, quality components that have held up quite well even after the passing of more than 60 years. Heavy cast metal bases, tops, and framework highlight beautifully composed scenes adhered to glass. Rich colors and detailed art work prevailed. Their lamps set standards that producers of lamps would follow from that time on. We would even go so far as to say that many of the motion lamps of later years were often imitations or inspirations based on Scene-in-Action lamps. Compare their 1931 Marine lamp to the 1956 Goodman Lighthouse and you'll see what we mean.

Judging by the number of Scene-in-Action lamps that have survived and turn up today, we know they were very popular in their time. The cylindrical lamps are the most common, since the 9½" tall lamps generally sold for $4.95. The metal framework lamps sold for $5.95 and are relatively abundant. But the Aquarium lamp sold for $7.95, and the top of the line glass table lamps sold for a whopping $14.95 (three times the price of the cylindrical lamps). Thus, the latter two are quite hard to come by today.

The cylindrical models also featured metal trays that sat on the rim of the glass, under the top. This allowed the user to place a few drops of perfume or incense mixed with water in the cup of the tray, filling a room with fragrance as the lamp operated. This feature added to their popularity. While most of their lamps included power switches as standard equipment, the cylindrical series, surprisingly, lacked them.

Scene-in-Action also produced large wood, metal, and glass lamps in the late twenties that were used for advertising. The impressive house fire lamp that was sold to insurance companies is exemplary. Without a doubt their oddest lamp is the burning cross, used in windows to mark Ku Klux Klan meetings. Luckily, we purchased our example of this rare lamp from a man who was embarrassed to own or display it.

Today's collectors often prefer the 1950s plastic lamps since they remember them better and are impressed with their relatively larger scene dimensions,

Old Scene-in-Action factory building as seen today at 1603 South Michigan.

14

but take our advice and don't ignore these beautifully crafted early lamps. They will, indeed, light up your life. And read the inspiring brochure written in 1931 for prospective customers, and you will find yourself drawn to their products just as people were over 66 years ago.

In this chapter, we document 14 standard lamps and nine specialty lamps they produced.

NATURE'S OWN COLORS

Moonlight

Design 45
Size 5½ x 9½   **$4⁹⁵**

THE lovely MOONLIGHT lamp illustrated above can truly be interpreted as "a masterpiece." When lighted, its special color effects produce an array of colors which might have been blended by Nocturn himself. To see this lamp compels one to dream of life at its most romantic moments. You may spend a peaceful night in a tropical, moonlit bay of glistening water right in your own home. It never becomes tiresome; its hypnotic effect satisfies the most skeptical. Complete with incense burner, bulb, silk cord and plug.

Colonial Fountain

Design 46
Size 10½ x 9¼   **$6⁹⁵**

BEAUTIFUL in design and color, the COLONIAL FOUNTAIN'S gentle spray never fails to command intense interest. The graceful fountain continuously spouts a gentle stream of phosphorescent water, which, as it again descends, is transformed into rainbow hues of mist. Surrounding the fountain is a beautiful colonial court backed by stately columns. In the background, huge southern pines rise in splendor against a flawless summer sky. The natural and lifelike color of this scene adds beauty and distinction to any room. Encased in a beautiful lightweight metal frame, finished in bronze. Complete with bulb, switch, silk cord and plug.

READ THIS—IMPORTANT

SCENE-IN-ACTION creations are distinctive, unique, appealing, decorative—the latest contribution to artistry in lighting. They brighten that dark nook, improve and beautify the radio, and decorate the mantel. The softly colored rays make them particularly adaptable for use as night lights. The small bulb permits their constant use, day and night, at a trifling cost. Designs No. 41, No. 43, No. 45 and No. 47 are equipped with perfume burners of unusual effectiveness. A few drops of your favorite perfume with an equal quantity of water will rapidly permeate an entire house. SCENE-IN-ACTION products operate on either AC or DC current.

COPYRIGHT 1931 BY SCENE-IN-ACTION CORP.

Marine

Design 47
Size 5½ x 9½   **$4⁹⁵**

THE MARINE design depicts two most realistic scenes of ocean beauty. The view above shows a ship at sea, sails full, waves breaking against its prow, blue skies above with billowing clouds drifting gently in the summer breeze. On the opposite side you see a jagged island of rocks, breakers pounding its sides, with a grim lighthouse towering above, flashing its warnings to ships that "pass in the night." You actually see all of this in action. It is a miniature motion picture in itself, and because of its perfect blending of colors and synchronized action, is a most realistic reproduction. Complete with incense burner, bulb, silk cord and plug.

The
Scene-in-action
Line
1931

REALISTIC SCENES - IN - ACTION

Forest Fire

Design 41
Size 5½ x 9½   **$4⁹⁵**

THE FOREST FIRE design is so realistic in color and action that you will hardly believe your eyes. You see a dense northern forest, stately pines, a hunter's cabin, a raging fire travelling at a terrific rate of speed, apparently destroying everything in its path, black smoke clouds rolling skyward. All this you actually see in action. It is a sight you will never forget, and a lamp you will want to own. Complete with incense burner, bulb, silk cord and plug.

Japanese Twilight

Design 42
Size 13¾ x 9   **$6⁹⁵**

THIS design is one of the most fascinating home lighting effects ever created. Turning on the switch, you behold a softly lighted scene depicting the tranquil waters of a hidden lake at the base of Fujiyama in its ageless glory, as seen through the eyes of an artist travelling in the Orient. You see the silver beams of a full Japanese moon reflected in the rippling water. This delightful scene is encased in a beautiful white metal frame of strictly modernistic design, finished in antique silver. Complete with switch, bulb, silk cord and plug.

GUARANTEE:

All SCENE-IN-ACTION products are manufactured of the highest grade non-inflammable materials obtainable. They are offered for sale only after SCENE-IN-ACTION engineers have completed exhaustive tests. Every one is assembled, thoroughly inspected and tested for defects before it is packed. The Scene-in-Action Corporation guarantees all of its products to be free of defective materials or workmanship.

PATENTS

SCENE-IN-ACTION products are manufactured and sold exclusively by the Scene-In-Action Corporation of Chicago under U. S. patents No. 1769751, No. 1761802, No. 75589, No. 1264416, and No. 195659. Canada, patents No. 197415 and No. 112756; Great Britain, patent No. 378195; France, patent No. 539234. The above patents are the property of the Scene-In-Action Corporation of Chicago, and in addition to those already granted patents are pending for additional improvements in the United States and all foreign countries of the world. Any Scene-In-Action or similar devices other than those manufactured by the Scene-in-Action Corporation, are not only unauthorized but are an infringement on the above exclusive patent rights. Infringers will be prosecuted to the fullest extent of the law. Scene-In-Action Corporation of Chicago.

The Serenader

Design 44
Size 13 x 11   **$6⁹⁵**

THE SERENADER is created from beautifully molded white metal, finished in antique bronze and gracefully set off by a panel of ground-edged glass. It pictures a dreamer's castle in the air, with a pool of glistening water. When lighted, it gives forth a blend of colors never before produced. We call special attention to the fineness in design of metal and glass. If you appreciate statuary bronze, you will want this for the lifelike detail of the base. Rippling moonlight rays, concerted with shifting shadows, create untiring interest. Complete with switch, silk cord and plug.

WHAT IS SCENE-IN-ACTION? SCENE-IN-ACTION is a new and original means of endowing beautiful pictures with color, life and movement. All SCENE-IN-ACTION creations are illuminated from behind, and even without motion would attract by their arresting beauty. The action, furnished by an amazingly simple but effective device, gives a sparkle of animation and beauty to the scene which increases its attractiveness a hundredfold. The mechanical construction of a SCENE-IN-ACTION device is very simple. There are no intricate parts to get out of order. Each model is packed in a separate container designed to conform with the requirements of all carriers. Instruction sheet for complete assembly is enclosed with each unit. SCENE-IN-ACTION products are the most novel and very latest means of attaining electrical beauty.

Niagara Falls

Model 43
Size 5½ x 9½   **$4⁹⁵**

THIS NIAGARA FALLS lamp brings to your home a true, colorful reproduction of the great Niagara in action. You see the River above peacefully travelling its course, Canadian hills in the background, and Goat Island in its prominence dividing the two greatest Falls in the world—the American and Canadian Niagara. When the lamp is lighted you see this majestic body of water surging to the rocks below, the rising spray with its rainbow hues painting in a summer sun, the historic Maid o' the Mist winding through the turbulent waters of the whirlpool, as the roaring river settles down in its course of travel below the Falls. All of this you actually see in action, just as you saw it on your trip to Niagara Falls. It is so different, so entrancing and natural in its action effect that you will stare in amazement. You will want to bring this world wonder to your home. Complete with incense burner, bulb, silk cord and plug.

LAMPS THAT HAVE LIFE AND COLOR

TABLE LAMPS
Nos. 48 and 49
Retail Price $14.95

BEAUTIFUL, uniquely designed table lamps with SCENE-IN-ACTION built into the base. No. 48 in black portrays a merchant schooner burning at sea after an attack by pirates, and on the opposite side, a blazing forest, a deer and its young pressed to the water's edge, trapped.

No. 49 in green, depicts a young cavalier scene —swans swimming about the edge of a stately fountain; on the opposite side, a romantic moonlight scene—a young cavalier with his lady love, beautiful moonlight rays beating gently on a Spanish fountain and its pool.

All of this you see in action and natural color. Complete with action bulb, silk cord, switch, plug and shade. Stands 24¾ in. high. Weight, fifteen lbs. packed.

PATENTS

SCENE-IN-ACTION products are manufactured and sold exclusively by the Scene-in-action Corporation, Chicago, Illinois. All SCENE-IN-ACTION products are manufactured under one or more of the following patents: U. S. Patent Numbers 1369751, 1761802, 1195659, 1308415, 1341201, 1492472, 1714717, 1719939, 1752014, 1805209, 1821538, 1821557, 1263391, 75589, 84165, 84166, 84167; Canadian Patent Numbers 113756, 197145, 221584, 285784, 299788; Belgium Patent Number 347137; Great Britain Patent Numbers 178195, 267460, 331262; France Patent Numbers 530234, 614810. Other patents pending. The above patents are the property of the Scene-in-action Corporation, and in addition to those already granted, patents are pending in the United States and all foreign countries of the world. Any SCENE-IN-ACTION or similar devices other than those manufactured by the Scene-in-action Corporation are not only unauthorized, but are an infringement on the above exclusive patent rights. Infringers will be prosecuted to the fullest extent of the law. (Signed) Scene-in-action Corporation, by Albert Sabath, President.

A RICH ORNAMENT FOR ANY ROOM

AQUARIUM No. 50
Retail Price $7.95

DISTINGUISHED from all other forms of animated lighting effects, the above aquarium must be seen to be appreciated. The metal base is beautifully finished. The pedestal, equipped with SCENE-IN-ACTION, enables you to visit the ocean depths. You see submarine life in its natural state — mammoth fish swimming about, ocean currents briskly churning a sandy bottom, and every natural color brought out to its best advantage. The two-gallon bowl on the pedestal has a transparent crystal rock in its bottom. Colored light rays, projected from the bulb below, throw myriads of reflected colors on the fish. Equipped with bulb, switch, silk cord and plug. Size 12"x14". Weight, nineteen lbs. packed.

SCENE-IN-ACTION
GUARANTEED QUALITY IN EVERY LAMP

All SCENE-IN-ACTION products are manufactured of the highest grade non-inflammable materials obtainable. They are offered for sale only after SCENE-IN-ACTION engineers have completed exhaustive tests. Every one is assembled, thoroughly inspected and tested for defects before it is packed. The Scene-in-action Corporation guarantees all of its products to be free of defective materials or workmanship.

Forest Fire (1931) #41

Fire blazes throughout the forest and nearby cabin.

Possibly the best fire effect created by a motion lamp. A best seller in its time, judging by the examples that are available today. Heavy, quality metal and glass construction is the norm as in all Scene-in-Action lamps. Although most metal work is composed of iron, occasionally lead composition metal work will be found in the round lamps. The weight and finish will identify lead examples. $125.00 – 175.00.

Niagara Falls (1931) #43

Water falls, churns, and moves downstream.

A bit harder to find than their Forest Fire, and not quite as realistic, but a fine lamp if found with brilliant original colors. Colors prone to fading or darkening to a brownish tint. This lamp gave birth to dozens of Niagara Falls models that followed. Cylinder color tends to fade, causing less defined animation. (See chapter on restoration to correct this problem.) $125.00 – 175.00.

Marine (1931) #47

*Waves rush over shore onto lighthouse and beacon flashes in different colors
while water below ripples. Rear shows waves moving beneath sailing ship.*

Sold in far less quantity than their Forest Fire and Niagara Falls, judging by examples that surface today. Beautiful if found with original colors and shiny surface glaze. More susceptible to fading than most. It is interesting that Goodman probably borrowed this design for their Lighthouse lamp. A rare deco framework is a variation that is nickel plated and bears the patent number 1369751-1761802. $225.00 – 275.00, more for nickel model.

Moonlight (1931) #45

Water in lake ripples gently.

Commonly called Moon and Lake. Beautiful to look at, but very scarce today since the subtle animation probably kept it from being a good seller in the 1930s. Both sides are similar. Japanese Twilight (pg. 22) also features a moon over a lake, but adds Mt. Fuji to the setting. Being more panoramic and much easier to find, that lamp may satisfy those looking for Moonlight. Animation sleeve tends to flake more on this model. The metal framework on this example has an unusual black and gold factory finish and a built-in power switch. What might have been a rare accessory was found with an example of this model — an incense cup the size of a silver dollar which fits into the standard incense tray for additional liquid capacity. $275.00 – 350.00.

Buddha (1931)

*Fire burns in the lap of Buddha, and as smoke rises, a
fountain pours to his right while water in lake ripples.*

Features the same scene front and rear and is the only
Scene-in-Action lamp that does. Reading original patent information reveals that the animated smoke effects would continue
as real smoke out of the metal top when the incense tray was
used in a certain manner to create smoke. Richly drawn graphic.
Extremely scarce. $350.00 – 400.00.

Flames (1931) #51

*Pirate ship is on fire with river flowing in one scene.
A forest fire blazes in second and third scenes.*

Interesting pagoda-like shape, and one of only two
lamps they produced that used plastic panels instead of glass
in front of the paper scenes. Subtler animation due to small
picture area. Usually found in copper finish, and sometimes
in the rarer chrome. Fairly hard to find. $200.00 – 275.00.

Ripples (1931) #52

*Man serenades lady by a tiered fountain in one scene.
A lake ripples (similar to Moonlight model) in the second
scene, and waves lap at vessels in the third scene.*

The unusual pagoda framework is featured. Available in copper finish and the rarer chrome finish. Like Flames, uses plastic window panels and came supplied with dark gray dual cardboard ring with holes in it that was adjustable to control air flow and thereby regulate cylinder speed. This device sat above the animation sleeve. Both pagoda shaped lamps divide action into three small sections, resulting in more subtle motion. Buyers then (and often now!) tended to favor larger animation areas, and sales of these lamps reflected this as they are hard to find today. A late model, made when Rev-o-lite took over the reins, features a graniteware-like finish, no plastic window panels, and no black framing of the scenes. $200.00 – 275.00.

"1933 Chicago World's Fair" (1933)

Fireworks flare and dissipate in two colors while tram car moves across the bridge and water ripples below.

The only lamp ever to attempt fireworks animation successfully. Extremely scarce. Released in glass and metal top framework and also in metal pagoda shaped framework. The later style reveals less picture area. Released in an unusual aluminum framework without the fireworks animation. Also found in Rev-o-lite framework. $350.00 – 400.00.

Japanese Twilight (1931) #42
Water ripples gently in the lake before Mount Fuji, and moon glows.

Smart Art Deco framework, finished in silver, and a panoramic scene made this a popular choice then and now. Tranquil to watch when lit and beautiful even when off. Not too difficult to find. Also released in a seldom seen three quarter size framework, with a textured, blackened front finish. $200.00 – 250.00, a bit higher for the framework that is two inches narrower.

Colonial Fountain (1931) #46
Fountain shoots water up and spray varies at top, then water flows down causing ripples below.

Beautiful Victorian style framework in bronze color shows man and lady standing before motion scene. This placement gives a three dimensional effect. Popular then and now, but harder to find than Japanese Twilight. Also available in very scarce pewter finish. This is a beautiful lamp that dealers often try to sell for higher prices even if not complete, as it is also nice as a non-animated lamp. Rear compartment tops were unattached and may be missing with the passing years. $250.00 – 300.00.

Serenader (1931) #44

Water in lake ripples while skyline glows.

Truly great lamp from its bronze-colored gondola framework to its heart-shaped glass and haunting scene. Guaranteed to please. Some models do not illuminate the skyline, but rather have a moon that glows, which is captivating but more subtle. With this style, the animation glass is a bit different to allow for the moon glow effect and the glass is colored black instead of blue. Both styles use a lamp compartment cover that is not attached. Somewhat hard to find. $350.00 – 400.00.

Aquarium (1931) #50

Water moves around fish in deep sea setting.

Unique design, as the motion lamp base supports a large glass fishbowl above. It was supposed to keep real fish at a good temperature. Priced higher than their regular lamps, it sold in much lesser quantities. Very scarce today and extremely hard to find with original "crystal rock" bottom on fishbowl. Action is out of the ordinary, as the water moves instead of the fish. Also shown with the flat bottom fishbowl. $450.00 – 550.00.

Table Lamp: Black Glass Model (1931) #48
Front side has a pirate ship on fire, with water flowing under ship at dock.
Rear side shows forest fire with stream running by deer in foreground.

Both graphics are larger versions of scenes used in their Flames lamp. Easily the Rolls-Royce of motion lamps, as it sold for $14.95 — three times the price of standard Scene-in-Action lamps of the time! Keep in mind how significant that amount was in the 1930s, when it represented a full weekly salary of an average worker. The lovely urn-shaped glass is colored black from within and framed by a matching cast metal base and metal top. Two sockets on the post above are for standard lamp illumination with pull chains for each. Turn the switch on the base once to light the standard lamp, turn it again for the motion unit, and turn it one more time to light both simultaneously. The cylinder and bulb are accessed by raising the metal top. Very scarce. $500.00 – 600.00.

Table Lamp: Green Glass Model (1931) #49

Front side features two ladies near a tiered flowing fountain with water rippling below. Rear side shows a man serenading his lady at a similar fountain (the same scene used in their Ripples lamp, only larger).

All information pertaining to Black Glass model on the previous page applies, but the Green Glass model is even harder to find today. Also, finding an original matching paper shade would be quite an accomplishment. Check original advertising literature to see shade size and design. $600.00 – 750.00.

Scene-In-Action Specialty/Advertising Lamps

The following lamps produced by Scene-in-Action were not sold to the public but were made for companies and specialty groups for advertising purposes. They are therefore much harder to come by than mass-produced lamps, making them quite special for private collectors with the space to house these generally much larger units. Specialty lamps will follow regular production lamps in each succeeding chapter.

"House Fire and Fire Engine" (1920s)

Flames blaze out of the house while jets of water pump through hoses and smoke billows from antique fire engine.

Sturdily made of wood, metal, and glass, this is a very impressive motion unit. It features one of the rarer uses of water pumping through a hose and may be the very first lamp to use this effect. It is quite large and houses two big cylinders that spin to produce the action. There are only a handful of lamps that use more than one cylinder turning in separate spaces. This lamp was probably used in insurance offices to sell fire insurance. It may have had a sign mounted above the unit for more information. A variation of this shows the same graphics except there is a "modern" fire engine on the left that has no animation and thus only one cylinder (for the flame effects). The variation appears to have been factory altered, as the newer graphic seems to be added over the original. Rare. $450.00 – 550.00.

"Start Saving Now" (1920s)

A speedboat churns the water while a message trail behind a plane flying above.

Both the same sturdy construction and dual cylinders featured in the preceding lamp are found in this lamp. The message says "Start Saving Now," so this was probably used by a bank. The graphic is quite colorful and inviting, while the motion is very natural and has the quality one would expect from this company. Rare. $400.00 – 500.00.

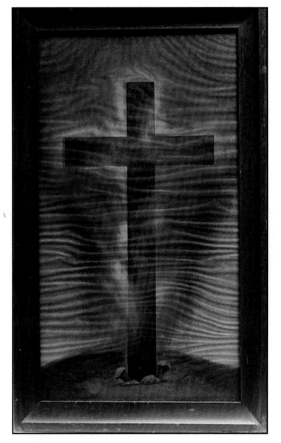

"Ku Klux Klan" (1920s)

A large cross burns.

While using the same sturdy construction featured above, this lamp has a huge cylinder that is powered by two 150 watt bulbs that sit on top of each other. The bulbs have a special design in that they are both clear and also partially frosted for the best effect. A large unit (17½" x 28½") that is quite impressive to see, as it is very realistic. One can imagine the effect it must have had sitting in a window at a Klan meeting. Rare. $600.00 – 750.00.

"Forest Fire Advertising Lamp" (1920s)

The fire blazes through the forest and smoke billows from the cabin's chimney.

Features similar construction as above. Was probably used by the department of forestry as a warning against forest fires. Rare. $400.00 – 500.00.

"Forest Fire Display Lamp" (1930s)
Fire blazes through the forest.

A huge replica of the standard Scene-in-Action forest fire lamp that stands 30" tall and is 17" in diameter. Probably used by the company in window displays to promote sales of their standard lamps. Very rare. $550.00 – 650.00

"Stewart-Warner Radio Display" (1920s)
Radio waves beam out of the broadcasting tower.

Another large and sturdily constructed unit that will appeal to radio collectors as well as lamp people. The animation is more subtle than most of the other Scene-in-Action specialty lamps, but the graphic is as appealing as any. Rare. $450.00 – 550.00.

"U. S. Leviathan Cruise Ship" (1930s)

Water moves under ship and name of ship is projected above and appears and disappears while the lighthouse beacon flashes and water spills around the lighthouse. Also, smoke pours from the stacks and a flag carrying the cruise line logo waves at the top of the lamp.

The graphic contains the wording "US Lines and American Merchant Lines." We obtained this from a man who told us that his father bought it from a travel agency that used it as far back as the 1930s. It is the same shape and construction as the standard Scene-in-Action round lamp, but over twice the size. Possibly one of the rarest lamps we have ever come across, it has animation that dazzles and is the kind of find we all dream about. The only identification was a tiny fragment of a decal on the bottom with the company name. $600.00 – 700.00.

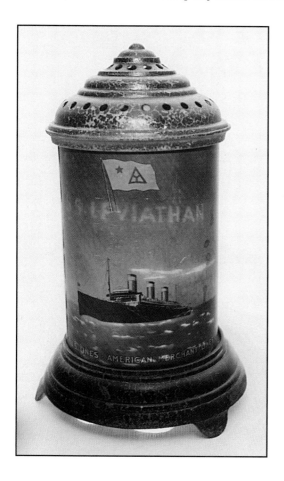

"Toasted Frankfurters" (1920s?)

Steam rises from hot dogs and a food platter, and the words "toasted to your order" project through.

The 4" x 7" frame makes this one of the smallest specialty lamps. Effective steam animation makes this tiny beauty interesting. Rare. $350.00 – 450.00.

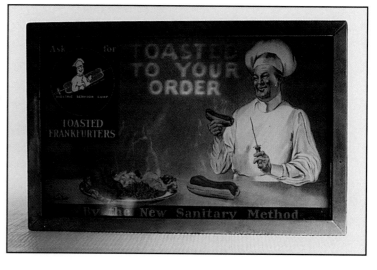

"Anti-Prohibition Lamp" (1930s)

Beer flows into glass. It reads "Beer for prosperity–repeal the 18th Amendment."

A gem of a piece since it is part of our country's history. It is the only Scene-in-Action product we have seen that is made of cardboard and paper, so it is particularly delicate at this age. Rare. $350.00 – 450.00.

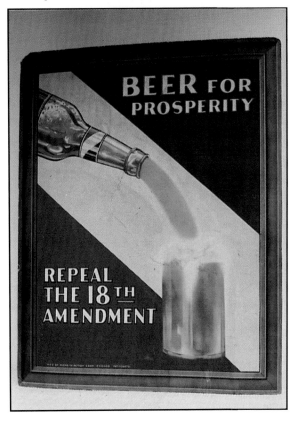

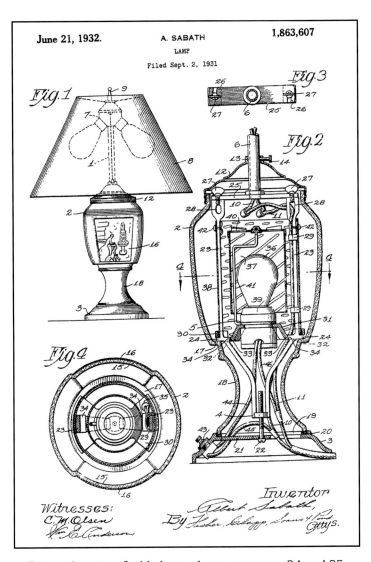

Patent drawing of table lamp shown on pages 24 and 25.

As this book went to press, we discovered a rare color advertisement for the return of the Scene-in-Action Forest Fire and Niagara Falls lamps (p. 17). Using the original company name, this "new" company in 1946 was offering nearly identical looking lamps people could order on approval without even sending money for the 1931 price of $4.95. In addition to calling themselves the "Scene-in-Action Lamp Co.," they used a subname, Rapids Specialties Company, located in Michigan. The most noticeable difference between their lamp and an original was the use of gold-colored plastic for the base and top. When you ordered, you received free a "wonder leaf," a plant that grows on air and needs no water. Our question is where are they today? We have never seen or heard of these before.

❧ National Company ❧

These lamps, produced in Canada during the 1930s, are obvious offshoots of Scene-in-Action products, judging by similar scenes and frameworks. A paper label on a rare lamp gave a clue to a possible licensing agreement between the two companies. The label reads "Scene-in-Action Lamp. Manufactured by National Picture Frame and Art Co., Ltd. Distributed by National Lamp and Elec. Co." Rugged, quality construction prevailed at National, resulting in durable products. The most obvious difference between output of the two companies was the construction of the bulb compartment lids. Generally, the National bulb compartment lids are somewhat more inconvenient than the Scene-in-Action lids since they have to be carefully fit to stay in place. Also, the scenes and frameworks are slightly smaller in size and therefore parts cannot be interchanged between lamps of the two companies. National produced some unique motion graphics that are quite worthy of collector attention. They are not common in this country, so develop friends in Canada who

can help you find them! To their credit, National used metal fans for their cylinder tops, a more durable choice than the treated paper tops produced by Scene-in-Action. And some of the polished, bronze finished highlights on the frameworks are strikingly beautiful. All National lamps are powered by 20 watt bulbs, most are equipped with power switches, and most use metal and glass construction. Small name decals inside identify them, unlike the metal stampings on Scene-in-Action lamps. Many originally had small, thin cardboard title strips glued to the metal fronts which had the official name of the lamp printed in black lettering. One example is "Off Dartmouth." Unfortunately, these are often missing with the passing years. We have found that animation sleeves or panels produced strictly by National (i.e., ones having no Scene-in-Action counterparts) generally do not provide as high a level of realism when lit. This is probably due to less refined stenciling. The quality of the paint used seems to be equal, though use of color differed. They produced 16 lamps that we document, but there are surely more that we hope will turn up in the future.

Off Dartmouth (1930s)

Crests of the waves glisten and ripple, a unique action since most other lamps feature wave motion rather than emphasizing the crests.

Features a name card glued to front (often missing) and nice bronze accents on the framework. Colors on National lamp graphics are often faded to some degree, perhaps with age and less stable color dies used. This example features better color than found on most. Scarce in U.S. $250.00 – 300.00

"Sailboat at Dock" (1930s)

Waves ripple as setting sun shines.

Better than average National lamp with interesting wave motion. Instead of the typical bronze finish, this example has a jazzy chrome plated front that is a standout. Also released in bronze. Scarce in U.S. $250.00 – 300.00.

"Windmill at Coastline" (1930s)

Waves move to the shore.

One of the prettiest National lamps with its finely detailed scene. Windmills are so appealing with their rustic charm. It's too bad there is no motion at this focal point. Scarce in U.S. $275.00 – 325.00.

"Battleship at Sea" (1930s)

Waves ripple and steam emanates from ship smokestacks.

A bold image with very subtle steam animation. The shading of the copper-colored highlights on the bronze-colored framework varied in shape and pattern on National lamps. Fairly scarce in U.S. $275.00 – 325.00.

"Winter Scene" (1930s)

Water ripples at a cabin by a lake in a snow-filled setting while smoke seeps out of the chimney.

Uses the Japanese Twilight framework but is slightly smaller in size. This is the only metal and glass winter scene of which we are aware to date. It is a shame they used the same water effects found on so many of their other lamps rather than snow falling. Very scarce in U.S. $300.00 – 350.00.

Nature's Splendor (1930s)

A brook gently flows and ripples between trees in an autumnal setting.

One of the most colorful National lamps, it features a very subtle and quiet animation that is soothing. Very scarce in U.S. $300.00 – 350.00.

"Lighthouse at Sunset" (1930s)

Waves crash on rocks at shoreline as the sun glistens on water to the right.

While the lighthouse is in the far distance unlike most other lamps featuring a lighthouse, the graphic focuses your attention onto the vivid ocean setting. Very scarce in U.S. $300.00 – 350.00.

"Sailing Ship" (1930s)
Waves move under ship.

Uses the Colonial Fountain framework but is slightly smaller in size and uses the same ship as featured on the rear of the Scene-in-Action Marine model. Quite scarce in U.S. $275.00 – 325.00.

"Metal Niagara Falls" (1930s)
Water falls and flows downstream.

Uses the same framework as Colonial Fountain. An effective motion scene due to the wide expanse of the falls and a fascinating water motion that has currents running toward the center from both sides. A chrome framework release includes a colorful decal that says "Roberval" which is probably the area in which it was originally sold. Scarce in U.S. An olive-colored framework with a different view of the falls is very unusual. $250.00 – 300.00.

"Wood Frame Niagara Falls" (1930s)
Water falls and flows downstream.

The same lamp as the previous entry, but in gesso or plaster molded over a wood frame. Two different patterns exist as pictured, and the lamps vary slightly in rear compartment size and shape. See More Motion Sickness chapter for a third style. Scarce in U.S. $250.00 – 300.00.

"Round Niagara Falls" (1930s)
Water falls and flows downstream.

From a distance, a viewer would think this is exactly like the round Scene-in-Action Niagara lamp, but looking closer reveals many differences. First, the scene has a distinctly different and more detailed "Maid of the Mist" boat. Overall color is softer, but this is probably due to fading. Looking at the pivot post reveals a different mounting system. The design details on the metal surfaces are bolder and have less fine detail, and like all other National lamps, there are copper-colored highlights. The bottom of the base is stamped "N F P," which must stand for National, and has corresponding patent numbers. There is an on-off switch and a hole for the wire to run through on the base. The cylinder and animation sleeve are very different in graphic design. The end result is animation that is more vivid and more realistic than the Scene-in-Action counterpart. The round Nationals are seldom seen, in fact this example was found only weeks before the final draft of this book. We would speculate that a forest fire version also exists. Very scarce in U.S. $175.00 – 225.00.

Mayflower (1930s)
Waves move and ripple under the famous vessel.

Another gesso frame lamp. Very scarce in U.S. $275.00 – 325.00.

"Japanese Twilight" (1930s)

Similar to the Scene-in-Action model of the same name, but differs in size and finish. Scarce in U.S. $225.00 – 275.00.

"Colonial Fountain" (1930s)

Similar to the Scene-in-Action model of same name, but differs in size and has more copper highlights on its front. A more noticeable difference is the animation which is less refined but yields a richer and more "gutsy" look to the water flow. Scarce in U.S. $250.00 – 300.00.

"Jesus Christ on the Water" (1930s)

Water moves under Christ's feet.

The gesso-covered wood frame is finished in gold. A lovely lamp depicting a Biblical scene. A collector may find many illuminated religious scenes but few that have motion. Also released in non-gesso smooth wooden frame. Very scarce in U.S. $275.00 – 325.00.

"Fisherman by Sailboats" (1930s)

Water ripples.

Uses a wooden frame and a scene printed on cardboard. The cardboard blocks light too much, making what could have been a fine lamp look rather dull except in a very dark environment. Scarce in U.S. $200.00 – 250.00.

"Serenader with Pine Trees" (1930s)
Water falls.

Beautiful graphics and the fine Serenader framework in a lamp that has very subtle motion. Features a black finish on the metalwork. Very scarce in U.S. We have come across two Serenader examples with a painted finish that includes what looks like Niagara Falls animation glasses in a brown color. The yellow cylinders include what looks like water lines at bottom and fire lines at top. Furthermore, both examples have an upside down forest fire graphic on the lower portion of the scene glass, while the upper portion is just clear (that is, there is no scene pasted on). The lamp has no meaning when operating; it appears incomplete. Our first impression when receiving this lamp was that it was tampered with until we saw photos of an identical piece! If anyone out there can help solve this mystery, please contact us. $325.00 – 375.00.

❦ Rev-o-Lite ❦

With quality construction matching the fine pagoda-shaped Scene-in-Action lamps, Rev-o-lite produced lovely pieces in the 1930s. Framework was metal with plastic-covered windows and plastic cylinders topped with metal fans. They were priced at $4.95 each. Rev-o-lite lamps were released in varied and beautiful finishes that make them stand out distinctively today. Based in New Brunswick, New Jersey, at the corner of George and Hamilton Streets, they later opened an office in Chicago, Illinois, at 4951 West 65th Street. In 1936 the president was F. N. Manley, and in 1937 the president was R. W. Johnson. By 1938 there was no longer a corporate listing for them. The company produced nine lamps that we document. Only two of these have true animation, and they are the models that have Scene-in-Action parts (see chapter on Scene-in-Action). Most of their lamps feature graphics on a cylinder that surrounds an inner scene. The cylinder revolves around the scene with a carousel-like action. Some lamps are found with a dual metal incense tray that has two layers which move to control air flow as well as hold liquid, while others are found with a dual cardboard sleeve for air flow control only. All lamps have adjustable peaks at the top to further control air flow. While their lamps are subtle, they are nevertheless quite charming. Rev-o-lite released a compelling brochure describing their motion lamps. Review the text and pictures and then go out and try to find surviving examples. In general, they are much harder to locate than other lamps produced in the same time period so prize those you capture!

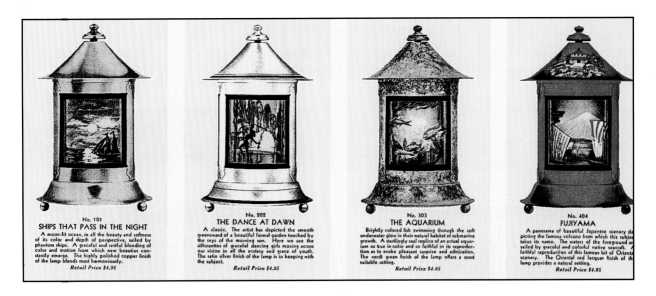

| No. 101 | No. 202 | No. 303 | No. 404 |
| SHIPS THAT PASS IN THE NIGHT | THE DANCE AT DAWN | THE AQUARIUM | FUJIYAMA |

Ships that Pass in the Night (1930s) #101
Black silhouettes of ships pass by a cloud and sea background.

Has three windows for viewing action. A scene printed on plastic or paper-covered plastic surrounds the bulb, while the images on a clear plastic cylinder rotate around the scene. This lamp was released in a copper finish. $200.00 – 250.00.

Dance at Dawn (1930s) #202
Black silhouettes of naked nymphs jumping rope in various poses pass by a pastoral scene.

This lamp was released in a satin finished silver color with black pin stripes. $200.00 – 250.00

Aquarium (1930s) #303
Colorful fish swim underwater, passing deep sea foliage.

This lamp was released in a Verdi green finish. An unusual variation employs a light green framework color and the use of a light green color to highlight the window openings, which are usually done in a black color. $175.00 – 225.00.

Fujiyama (1930s) #404
Brightly colored Oriental vessels navigate past the famous Mt. Fuji volcano.

This lamp was released in an Oriental red finish. $225.00 – 275.00.

Venice (1930s) #505

Black silhouette gondolas drift by a Venetian setting.

This lamp was released in a bronze finish. $200.00 – 250.00.

Fairy Tale Folk (1930s) #606

The Seven Dwarfs, Little Bo Peep, Little Red Riding Hood, and other characters move past the scene of Cinderella's castle.

Possibly the most beautiful Rev-o-lite due to the colors on the rotating cylinder and the unusual texture on the golden brass finish which imitates a frost-like pattern. $250.00 – 300.00.

"Niagara Falls" (1930s)

Water flows and runs downstream.

Uses the same scene and inner parts as the Scene-in-Action Niagara Falls. One of two Rev-o-lite lamps to use true animation. Rather scarce. $175.00 – 225.00.

41

"Flames" (1930s)

Uses the same scenes and inner parts found in the Scene-in-Action lamp of the same name, but is housed in a brass Rev-o-lite framework. One of two Rev-o-lite lamps to use true animation. Curiously, there is no clear plastic covering the scenes, which exposes them to easy damage. Still another variation of this lamp has the scenes pasted to thin cardboard, yielding a sturdier but duller scene area. Rather scarce. $225.00 – 275.00.

"1933 Chicago World's Fair" (1933)

A dirigible, speedboat, and top wing single engine monoplane pass by the scene of the fairground.

The Century of Progress decal appears on top of the lamp. A crossover collectible that is extremely scarce today. $375.00 – 425.00.

A typical Rev-o-lite name decal underneath the lamp.

Econolite Corporation

The majority of motion lamp collectors would probably agree that Econolite made their favorite lamps. Based in Los Angeles, California, they produced more lamps than any other company. We can document over 80 standard lamps and six specialty units. They were in production from 1946 to 1963, a longer time than any other motion lamp company. And they still exist today, but they do *not* make motion lamps. With gleaming brass plated bases and top quality lithography and silk screening, their action scenes rose above the ordinary. Among the predominantly plastic lamps of their time, their construction was superior. Tight fitting seams, metal fans, careful scene alignment, and a wide variety of subject matter add much to their appeal.

The general office of the Econolite Corporation was located at 8900 Bellanca Ave., Los Angeles. Their Canadian office was located at 368 Dixon Rd., Toronto 15, Ontario. (No wonder they turn up in that country today!) The lamp division existed at 3517 West Washington Blvd., Los Angeles. Artist and designer Aubrey B. Leech was chief of Econolite's lamp and lithograph division. His signature is often seen on the lamps of the late 1940s and right on through to the 1960s. Nearly all Econolite lamps are marked with production and model numbers, so the job of documenting them has been made easier. Note that when purchasing an Econolite today, it is wise to check the cylinder number against the number on the animation sleeve. If the numbers match, you are assured of buying a complete lamp. The wrong cylinder inside will disappoint and lower value, while often ruining or lessening the animation effects.

Their lamps sold from a low of $2.95 for paper revolving Christmas trees to a high of $7.95 for the most detailed children's lamps. The standard cylindrical or oval lamps sold for $5.95. The earliest models were often children's lamps (such as Mother Goose), and soon

Roto-Vue, Jr. lamps followed (like the Circus). While most of the children's lamps (from the carousel style to the Roto-Vue, Jr. style) were made in fairly limited quantities, the Roto-Vue, Jr. lamps targeting the adult market were produced in great quantities. They became very popular with their nicely shaped plastic tops and bases, and their suitable size allowed them to be placed just about anywhere. By the mid-1950s, the most often produced lamps were the large cylindrical ones most collectors covet, with many made in the oval format as well. To achieve the oval shape, they simply "squeezed" the lamp slightly to form an oval. If one looks straight on at any of their round lamps, 5½" of picture can be seen, while their oval lamps yield 6½" of picture area giving a somewhat more panoramic view. Some of today's collectors tend to prefer oval style for this reason, but be prepared to find fewer available lamps in this format. By the late 1950s, the oval shape became the only shape used until production ceased.

Both shapes used the same brass-plated bases with the familiar "chain link" pattern. The majority of lamps you see will have this pattern (pictured on the front cover of this book as a background graphic). Two other extremely scarce base patterns exist. One features an angular, geometric pattern, while the other has a circular scheme. All standard bases included black ball feet that were made originally from wood and made later using black colored plastic.

For a short time in the mid-1950s, Econolite experimented with a picture frame style lamp series that apparently did not sell as well as the standard lamps, judging from the examples that turn up today. They were priced at $1.00 more, which may also account for their lesser sales. These lamps are more subtle and somewhat more fragile than other Econolites. They were named Living Pictures (with LP model numbers) since the idea was a picture that comes to life when the switch is turned on.

Be very careful when handling Econolite lamps today. The type of plastic used has hardened with age and the lamps can and will crack like glass when dropped on a hard surface. (Goodman lamps will usually bounce back into shape when dropped.)

Generally speaking, oval Econolite lamps are harder to find than their round counterparts. Also, lamps made from 1959 and after are harder to find than mid-1950s models. Lamps made from 1961 to 1963 are toughest of all to locate, as considerably fewer were produced until all production ceased. Size-wise, here is the lineup: Roto-Vue, Jr. lamps stand 9½" tall, the picture frame lamps are 10" inches, standard lamps are 11" inches, and pedestal base models are 14".

A little known fact is that most Econolite lamps were printed on *both* sides of the outer shade surface. This practice yielded richer colors to the lighted images. And there is an interesting plus for today's collectors — if the outer scene is faded, turning the lamp on will result in better color since the colors are projecting from within where fading does not occur. Moreover, a sharp eye can detect fine differences in color registration of Econolite lithos. They will vary from razor sharp to very soft or even out of focus when looking at them up close.

Looking closely at the fine print containing identification information for Econolite lamps, the phrase "hand printed" sometimes appears on the shades and cylinders. Hand printed (we assume this means not machine printed) lamps can be prized or scorned by today's collectors since they varied so much in their finished look. Some, like the 1962 Truck and Bus, offer finer color subtleties, while others like the 1955 Niagara Falls look washed out. Generally speaking, the litho quality is somewhat more grainy, but not always, as the hand printed 1955 Forest Fire will prove. Furthermore, some of the later lamps marked "hand printed" look identical to their standard litho counterparts which totally confuses the issue. The phrase "beauty is in the eye of the beholder" is our only answer to the dilemma.

At the end of this chapter, take note of Econolite's special series of lamps, which they called Scenes-in-Action (we wonder who was their inspiration!) or motion-in-advertising. Artists were willing and able to create custom-made lamps for diverse companies who realized the unique advantages offered by advertising that used motion. The vivid lasting impressions left by this form of advertising delighted clients and consumers alike. A few pages from their brochure provide an interesting background to the workings of the Econolite Corporation's Specialty Lamp Division. This unit actually produced motion-in-advertising billboard signs in 1938, predating Econolite standard lamp production by eight years. A sign released showing a plane in flight (complete with moving clouds and turning propellers) may have had its roots in the 1920s Scene-in-Action specialty lamp called "Start Saving Now." While the billboard type of construction required motorized animation for stability under outdoor conditions and was much more expensive to create, it caught on and became popular until our country's involvement in World War II. By then, shortages and blackouts caused the curtailment of the use of these huge advertising devices. However, after the war Econolite focused on creating motion advertising in display units that were far smaller and much easier to produce. For advertisers, this was quite appealing and therefore put Econolite into the forefront of this market (L.A. Goodman produced even smaller displays, but also took advantage of this marketing opportunity). For collectors, their output has provided unique motion displays to search out.

Motion in Advertising . . .

. . . With or Without Meaning?

by C. H. Chace

Vice President, Econolite Corporation, Los Angeles

IN the vast field of point-of-purchase advertising, there is nothing new in the practice of supplying movement to an attractive static display for the added advantage of its attention value. It is possible, however, that some advertisers have not fully recognized that there are two distinctly different types of movement as applied to attention value and advertising value. These might be explained as:

A. Mere motion without meaning, and,

B. Animation conveying intelligence.

Considering the original ideas and high-quality sales message delivered by most of the static point-of-purchase advertising, it can be argued that when motion is required, nothing more than a very inexpensive "attention-getting" movement is necessary to complete the selling job. Doubtless this is often true. However, products differ. Many do not lend themselves to animation at all, while others definitely require it for best results. Thus, when the display can be created to convey an intelligent understanding, such understanding can be often greatly enhanced if the picture is made to move with realism, with naturalness, and with intelligence.

Advertisers in the outdoor field use an established "circulation" formula for evaluating a bulletin location. Advertising executives, being familiar with the tremendous over-all volume and general breakdown of the many kinds of point-of-purchase advertising, have their own opinions as to what type of display is worth how much.

But, apparently, no formula has yet been developed that will properly evaluate the difference in advertising value between an animated display that merely moves and one that moves to convey an intelligent message.

The appraisal, therefore, would have to be a matter of individual opinion. But it is notable that when "motion with a message" is seen, its value is immediately recognized. It stimulates thought and understanding. It often produces on-the-spot sales.

Since 1938, the scene-in-action principle has been developed and a steadily increasing number of advertisers have been found who recognize the advertising value of realistic animation; buyers who are willing to pay the extra cost necessary to have it originated and produced. And while this type of animation has been supplied to practically all branches of the sign industry, it has done an outstanding job for point-of-purchase use.

For example, food or beverage displays—animated—must have definite appetite appeal, in addition to attention value. This means the origination of a good idea, plus realism . . . in motion and color. If grape juice is the subject, a picture of luscious grapes realistically dropping juice of the right color into a glass, will make almost anyone want to drink that juice. And if the display includes a background of a rolling-hills vineyard in bright sunshine, the idea of "sun-sweetened juice" will intelligently enhance the appeal.

Again, supposing the product is maple syrup in a bottle, a faithful reproduction of the bottle and label must also embrace the intelligent action of the syrup actually moving in a slow, curling-pour downward from the bottle to flow over an appetizing stack of cakes. If the melting butter can be also seen oozing over the side of the cakes, the appetite appeal is complete.

Of course, the same picture, without motion, would also be appetizing. But with realistic animation, its appeal becomes sensational and fascinating.

The very fascination of such a display impels customer interest; creates the definite completeness of understanding so ardently sought by any advertiser. Depending, of course, on the quality of the art, together with the general design, such a display becomes tops as a selling unit—practically a silent salesman. Obviously, the two descriptions given above serve the imagination with an almost unlimited variety of ideas possible to point-of-purchase animated displays; but one additional and very popular type of animation pouring beverage, such as beer.

Here again, the art must faithfully reproduce the bottle, the label, the glass and the correct color, of the beer. Then the animation is usually created to appear, realistically, in the neck of the bottle, the "pour" and in an agitation throughout the glass. The added feature is a "waving liquid line," at the bottom of the foam. This furnishes the crowning touch of thirst appeal; he final touch of realism that puts intelligence into the action. Each different subject therefore, must likewise depict some such outstanding degree of naturalness.

The mechanics of this type of animation require a technique embracing a combination of science and art. The picture may be produced in one of several ways, but in the form of a lithograph it must be printed with special inks on a special type of paper.

Basically, the science consists of light-projection and control. But the creation of such control as will produce action with intelligence, requires a most exacting technical skill. The spread of light rays from one lamp, projected through the picture, comprises the unit area of animation. As the size of the picture is increased, there will be a multiplicity of unit areas to be animated. This means a multiplicity of lamps and it means, further, that the rays of light from each will meet and cross at the same time they are put into motion; thus, they must be controlled so that the movement appearing on the picture will be in the right place, at the right time—and natural. If a moving train is being shown, for example, it must be kept on the track.

When a job of this kind is completed, the uninformed, looking at the physical aspects only, often confuse it with the ordinary globe sign. This is because globes are used as the sources of light. A casual observer may try to judge value by that standard. A few, even, have the idea that a so-called heat-motor and revolving cylinder placed in a cabinet back of any picture is all that is necessary to attain intelligent animation of that picture. Such attempts, however, quickly disclose a fallacy, although until this difference is understood, some advertisers make the error of grossly misjudging production costs.

Problems of this nature are today naturally overshadowed by the very unpredictable conditions resulting from the national emergency. The entire display industry is affected and its every branch is keenly interested in finding the manner in which it may make its own best contribution.

Considering the type of animation discussed in this article, it seems but a step to the field of visual-education in animation. In whatever size mav be required, this contribution takes the form of a schematic picture, in scale, which, by cutaways in the art work depicts in motion and color both the inside and outside operation of a mechanical device.

Mass of boiler tubes is revealed in this cut-away display for the Clayton Mfg. Co. By means of color and proper direction of flow, "Econolite" shows 18 different motions.

SUCH concerns as The Henry J. Kaiser Steel Co. of Fontana, Cal., and Combustion Engineering-Superheater, Inc. of New York are among many that have already used this type of animation extensively.

Their primary purpose has been to give their salesmen and their customers a better understanding of their product. For the Kaiser Co., the purpose was to convey an understanding of how steel is made. Thus. the motion showed the inside and outside operation of a gigantic blast furnace. For Combustion, the purpose was to depict the intricate direction and flow of forces within a huge steam generating plant—a plant that might cost millions of dollars to build.

This type of animation produces a visual impact which technicians and instructors have already recognized for the unusual value of the understanding it conveys. And while, for the purpose of education, such displays are often made in large size, numerous concerns use a small-size diagrammatic cutaway—animated—and produced in quantity as demonstration units for their salesmen.

As national production goes into high gear there is the ever-increasing problem of training novice employees efficiently and in the shortest time possible. Constancy of action in a training unit becomes a factor, since it allows the instructor to spend as much time as is necessary on each point. Too, this understandable, visual impact of the flow and direction of forces, offers to the student the greatest possible retention value.

Animation with intelligence, therefore, will join with all other branches of the display industry in making a worth-while contribution to the mobilization program. Whether in the form of educational exhibits of large size made in single units for training purposes among the armed services; for the training of industrial employees or for smaller units made in quantity and in point-of-purchase sizes for whatever purposes seem necessary, scientific animation can be expected to perform with intelligence and understanding.

Reprint from Point of Purchase Merchandising - March 1951

Reprinted from "Motion in Advertising," C.H. Chance, *Point of Purchase Merchandising.*

"Circus" (1958) #655

Dogs jump through a hoop, seals spin wheels and balls on their snouts, elephants shoot water from their trunks, a trumpet blasts out musical notes, a firecracker sparkles, and flaming torches burn.

Quite a few different actions and a striking graphic of a circus setting highlight this fine lamp. A unique design not found in any other known lamp, in that the upper area uses true animation while the lower portion uses a pleated inner sleeve for "distortion" animation featuring the dogs jumping. Very scarce. $350.00 – 400.00.

Hawaiian Scene (1959) #701

Multiple waterfalls flow between rock masses, then water flows downstream while clouds shift above.

One of three extruded shade models, featuring raised surface graphics. The oval scene areas are surrounded by palm trees and bamboo shoots to add to the exotic setting. Both sides are similar. Truly beautiful, hard to find, and sought after by Hawaiian collectors as well as lamp collectors. Recently featured in the movie *House Arrest* with Jamie Lee Curtis, but the lamp never showed any action. Maybe the cylinder was stuck! $350.00 – 400.00.

Oriental Garden (1959) #702

Waterfalls cascade, then water flows downstream as clouds shift on the horizon.

One of three extruded shade models. The oval scene area on the front side features an Oriental man and woman seated in a garden with waterfalls and stream surrounding them. The rear side is similar but has a bird flying and no people are pictured. A very beautiful lamp that has an unusual lime green surface color with trees and garden pagodas surrounding the scenes. Very hard to find. $350.00 – 400.00.

Bicycles (1959) #703

Ground moves underneath the bicycles, wheels revolve, and the countryside passes by in the background.

One of three extruded shade models. Prized for its beauty and striking action. Front side features a bicycle built for two, while the rear shows two high wheel bicycles. Each oval scene area is framed by a Victorian wall sconce with candles against a brick pattern background. Very hard to find. $350.00 – 400.00.

Fish (1954) #751, #752

Colorful tropical fish of various sizes and shapes swim by.

The pleated shade creates the effect of motion. Brilliant iridescent colors give the lamp its appeal. When the light is off, the fish are not visible. Produced on a standard base as well as a pedestal base. A rare variation of this lamp contains a cylinder with fresh water fish pictured. $175.00 – 225.00. Add $25.00 or more for rare cylinder.

Butterfly (1954) #753

Butterflies flutter by an outdoor setting.

The pleated inner sleeve creates the motion effect on the outer surface bearing foliage drawn in black images. Multicolored butterflies with an iridescent glow add to the beauty. They are not visible when the lamp is off. Interestingly, an "educational supplement" was supplied with the lamp that depicts and names each of the 15 different specimens. A few of the smaller specimens are duplicated, bringing the total featured to 22. Also released on pedestal base. Moderately easy to find. $150.00 – 200.00.

Cover Girls (1955) #754

The shade simply spins around.

The graphic features 12 beautiful girls as rendered by pin-up artist Gil Elvgren. Each girl has a double meaning caption under her image and each girl stands out in strong contrast to the dense black background. A crossover collectible with wonderful images to amuse and delight. Released on a pedestal base and actually called a Roto-Vue lamp. Relatively scarce. $400.00 – 450.00.

Venice Canal (1963) #757

On the front side, water ripples and glistens in Venice canal as clouds move above. On the rear side, Mt. Vesuvius erupts and lava flows down the mountain sides as water ripples in the foreground.

Sought after because of fetching artwork and color, but the subtle animation may disappoint. Only produced in the oval format. Very scarce, as it is one of the last lamps produced by Econolite. $350.00 – 435.00.

"Fountains of Versailles" (1963) #758

Water shoots up center of fountains, varying at height of tallest fountain, and cascades down in multiple streams on multiple levels, while water ripples below.

Released one year after Fountains of Rome and even rarer, since this was Econolite's last year in the lamp business. It was only released in the oval format. A brilliant use of water effects as the front side features the Pond of Latona and the rear features Apollo's Basin. (note that on the lamp itself, the basin is misspelled as Apoll's.) Uses the same cylinder as the Eiffel Tower lamp. Features dozens of individual water sprays, more than any other known lamp. $350.00 – 425.00.

"Eiffel Tower" (1963) #759

Six fountains spurt up and flow down before the famous Eiffel Tower and water flows at the Trocadero Gardens on the front while a two-tiered fountain pours and water ripples at the Place De La Concorde on the rear. Water also shoots upward from urns that are part of statues.

A remarkable lamp since it has so many fountains operating at once. Available only in the oval format and quite rare due to a very late release date. Uses the same cylinder as the Fountains of Versailles lamp. $450.00 – 500.00.

Forest Fire (1955) #761

Fire rages upward from trees while river flows downstream.

Rich colors and detailed graphics make this a very appealing lamp. Quite popular then and now. Released in round, oval, and hand printed formats. The hand printed model is exceptionally beautiful. $100.00 – 125.00.

Forest Fire (1960)

Fire rages in trees and a nearby stream flows.

A striking graphic, released only in the oval format, and hard to find due to a late release date. The dark and rather dense look gives the scene a setting at dusk. Note cabin in the foreground on both sides. Uses the same cylinder number as the 1955 model (761 B.O.), but the graphic is different. $175.00 – 225.00.

Niagara Falls (1955) #762

Water falls, churns, and bubbles at bottom, then flows downstream. In some models, clouds shift at the skyline.

A hugely successful lamp, judging by the large number that have survived. Realistic graphics. Released in round and oval formats, and both formats featured a blue skyline, a lesser seen pink skyline, or an even rarer orange skyline. Some hand-printed models were released as well. These featured a yellow skyline and a turquoise blue coloration with the Niagara Falls name in bold black letters. The movie *Liar's Edge* with Shannon Tweed takes place around Niagara Falls and includes nice shots of this lamp. $100.00 – 125.00. Slightly higher for less common models.

"Rainbow Niagara Falls" (1960) #762

Water moves with a serene sheeting action downwards, then flows shimmering across rocks.

A rainbow graces the front side. Arguably, the best waterfall effect Econolite achieved. The rear side is similar, but shows a power plant below. Released only in the oval format and fairly hard to find. Confusing use of the same model number as the 1955 version, although its cylinder is different. $150.00 – 200.00.

Train (1956) #763

Ground moves under tracks while wheels roll, fire and smoke billow out of stack,
steam flows from whistle, headlamp flickers, and houses and trees pass by on the right.

A truly classic lamp due to excellent graphics and six different actions. The historic "General" is featured on the front, and "John Bull" is featured on the rear. Released in round, oval, and hand-printed formats. Red colors are generally somewhat more brilliant on oval models. This is the lamp that became a movie star when Penny Marshall featured it in the December 1996 release *The Preacher's Wife* (at one point a close-up of it fills the entire screen!). Not too difficult to find. $200.00 – 225.00.

Steamboats (1957) #764

Water flows toward boats, while fire and smoke billow out of stacks. Steam emanates from pipes, and tiny flags wave in the wind.

The historic July 1, 1880 "Robert E. Lee" and "Natchez" steamboat race is presented with beauty and detail. Black men can be seen working on the rear side. Released in round and oval formats. Desirable lamp that is sometimes hard to find. The animation alignment of the tiny flags waving is often imprecise at this age. $200.00 – 250.00.

Old Mill (1956) #765

Waterfall in upper background flows downward while water cascades over paddle wheel and embankment, then flows downstream.

Popular when released and still sought after due to a lovely old mill and the idyllic country setting. Released in round and oval formats. Not difficult to find. $125.00 – 175.00.

Snow Scene – Church (1957) #767

Gentle snow falls on country scene.

Serene and relaxing to watch. Very popular with collectors. Church is prominent and its windows glow with orange light. Released in round, oval, and hand-printed formats. Hand-printed lamps feature a totally different color scheme of rich purples and blues, and of these some were printed very dense, giving a dark nighttime look. We have heard that custom-made snow scenes with individual churches printed on the scene were produced, but have never seen one. Not that hard to find, except in hand-printed versions. $175.00 – 225.00.

Snow Scene – Bridge (1957) #766

All comments about Snow Scene – Church apply, except this lamp has only a tiny church in the distance. It was not released in hand-printed format and is a bit harder to find than #767. Possibly released together with its sister model to please people not interested in the religious connotation. $175.00 – 225.00.

Antique Car (1957) #768

Ground moves under cars, tires revolve, and houses and trees pass in the background.

Front side features a 1914 Stutz Bearcat while the rear sports a 1912 Model T Ford. A desirable and exciting lamp for collectors. Red colors on Stutz are often faded to orange or even yellow. Released in round and oval formats. Oval versions feature more colorful and panoramic background motion. Earlier releases used gray animation sleeves instead of later white sleeves. The darker sleeves resulted in stronger animation. $200.00 – 225.00.

Miss Liberty (1958)
#769

Light beams up and out from Lady Liberty's torch. Water ripples, and smoke is released from stacks on the boats. On the rear side, light beams from the top of the Empire State building with similar boat and water action below.

A rare and desirable lamp and a crossover collectible. Original sales were probably low due to the rather subtle animation. We have found that using a #773 Fireplace lamp cylinder will enhance the general animation, but lessen the light beam effects. $350.00 – 450.00.

Waterski (1958) #771

Water flows under skiers, and jets spray out from the skis and boats while palm trees and coastline pass in the background.

A great and classic lamp, a must for action at its best, and a piece worthy to be in any collection. The front side has three skiers and the rear side has two. Very desirable and rather scarce. $400.00 – 475.00.

Sailing Ships (1958) #772

A storm at sea as rain pours on the three ships, and waves lap at their prows.

This is the only lamp Econolite released featuring rain. Includes "Old Ironsides," the "Mayflower," and Windjammer vessels. Some viewers feel birds can be seen flying from the ships upon close inspection. Released in round and oval formats and in a hand-printed oval version that looks grainy and overly blue, but curiously has the ships moving in the opposite direction. Somewhat scarce. $225.00 – 275.00.

Hearth (1958) #773

Logs are ablaze, embers glow, steam emanates from the cauldron and the teapot, and the spinning wheel turns.

Detailed graphics in a lamp that is sure to please. Most call this "Fireplace," but an original box that surfaced recently caused us to rename it. Front hearth features a dog sleeping while the rear one shows a cat sitting near the hearth Released in round and oval formats with some color variations in models. An example can usually be found with some searching. Note that we have discovered this lamp in a box marked "Signature Products-A division of Tamar of Los Angeles." Econolite may have distributed it in the oval format through this outlet using the same model number, 773-0. $200.00 – 250.00.

Jets (1958) #774

Exhaust pours from jet engines in the four featured airplanes while clouds roll by underneath.

Often called "Airplanes," this is a marvelous and great lamp and also a crossover collectible. Features the DC 8, the Caravelle, and the Comet on front side and a large 707 on the rear. Released in round and oval formats. Relatively scarce. $375.00 – 425.00.

Historical Fires (1959) #775 – 0

Fire and smoke rage from the buildings while water ripples in the river and smoke drifts from stack on small boat. Two hoses pump water up to flames on the Chicago side.

Features the great Chicago fire of 1871 on the front side. It is the only standard Econolite lamp to show water pulsing from hoses. The rear shows the great London fire of 1666. Released only in the oval format. A good example of the superior animation and design of the latter day lamps. Unfortunately scarce and prone to easy fading of red colors. $375.00 – 450.00.

Truck and Bus (1962) #776

*The road moves under the vehicles, tires turn and exhaust fumes
pour from the truck while the countryside passes by on right.*

A desirable and excellent lamp. Very hard to find today, as it was released so late. Released in the oval format in standard litho as well as in hand-printed version featuring diverse pastel colors. Features a Trailways Bus on the front and a freight truck on the rear. $375.00 – 425.00.

Lighthouse (1962) #777

Blue and white waves flow toward the shore while spray laps over the rocks near the lighthouse, and the beacon flashes in the tower.

Features a unique and smooth wave action not used in any other lamp. The wave graphics are included on the lower portion of the cylinder and project onto the shade. Desirable and very hard to find. Released in the oval format only, and in a hand-printed version. $350.00 – 400.00.

Bayou Boats (1962) #778

Water moves under the prow of the boat and the paddle wheel moves while flames emanate from the torches and steam comes out of the pipes, with fire and smoke billowing from the stacks. The rear has the same animation, less the torches.

Features a more close-up view of a vessel that is similar to one shown on the earlier lamp called "On the Bayou." Front of the lamp shows front view of the vessel while the rear shows the back view. This spatial approach is different from most other lamps. Very scarce due to a late release. $325.00 – 375.00.

"Fountains of Rome" (1962) #779

Water shoots up and down the center of the fountain and cascades in multiple streams on several levels while water ripples below and clouds shift above.

The variation in height of the center water stream is a striking effect found only on a few other lamps. Fairly rare due to a late release date. Released in the oval format only. The front side features St. Peter's Fountain, while the rear side features the Trevi Fountain. $350.00 — 400.00.

Fish Bowl (1960) #781
Tropical fish swim by.

Unique, compote-shaped design that uses its shape to create the pleated edges that provide the animation illusion and bear the scene of a mermaid, seahorse, and undersea foliage. A molded gold plastic top and base complete this lamp. Uses the same cylinder as the 1950s fish lamp. Extremely scarce. $275.00 – 325.00.

Mermaid (1960s) #782
Tropical fish swim by.

The pleated inner shade gives the illusion of animation. Color litho of mermaid and seahorse is printed on an outer plastic sleeve along with undersea foliage that appears on the front side while the rear side shows a diver and a sunken ship. Uses the same cylinder as the 1950s fish lamp. Released only in the oval format and extremely scarce. $300.00 – 350.00.

Pot Bellied Stove (1962) #900
Fire blazes on all four sides of stove while embers glow on the bottom.

A unique and desirable lamp, which is actually a full-sized standard Econolite cylindrical lamp that is surrounded by a molded, decorative antique stove framework and a fancy top. Realistic to the point that it could almost burn you if you got too close! A fascinating story will bear out that last remark. Recently our friend and lamp enthusiast Al Glasier ordered a Pot Bellied Stove lamp and tried it out by lighting it and setting it near his kitchen window. A few minutes later the fire department was banging on his door to put out the fire! It turns out one of the neighbors reported the fire after seeing the flames in Al's window. One of the bewildered firemen admitted that the flames were the most realistic he had ever seen in all his years of firefighting. The moral of the story is watch where you put those motion lamps, folks. Very scarce due to the late release date and also available in the even rarer silver-painted model that has black trim areas. $350.00 – 400.00. Add $50.00 or more for the silver model.

Ducks (1955) #953
Four tiers of colorful ducks flap their wings in flight, and water ripples below.

The setting features cattails in a marsh. Unique construction, with the spinning cylinder set between the animation sleeve and the outer shade. Released with a pedestal base for added height. Ducks are invisible when the lamp is off. Moderately hard to find. $200.00 – 275.00.

63

Mallards in Flight (1955?)

Four tiers of colorful mallards flap their wings in flight, and water drifts below.

Variation on Ducks lamp with a setting of pine trees. Water action at bottom features waves washing back from the shoreline. Released on a pedestal base, and one of the only Econolite lamps to feature natural walnut ball feet instead of the usual black feet. Much harder to find than Ducks. $225.00 – 300.00.

Seattle World's Fair (1962) #961

The famous Space Needle flame burns and glows various colors, light beacons emanate in different colors, and a tram car passes from left to right.

An impressive graphic made for the World's Fair in Seattle, Washington. Most unusual, since the rear side shows an aerial view of the fairgrounds but has no animation at all. This is the only Econolite lamp to have a rear scene that is not animated. Released only in the oval format, and scarce. A crossover collectible that is harder to find in the eastern U.S. $300.00 – 375.00.

"Picture Frame Forest Fire" (1953) #LP – 1/FF

Fire rages through the trees while water flows in the stream.

A wood frame and cardboard mat hold this picture that comes to life when the switch is turned on. Uses glass to protect the picture area, and uses glass behind the scene for the animation sleeve. Generally, picture frame lamps are hard to find. Often missing the rear cover flap which contains instructions for use. These lamps were meant to be placed on a shelf, and not on a wall as many people assume. $125.00 – 175.00.

"Picture Frame Niagara Falls" (1953) #LP – 2/NF

Water falls and churns, then flows downstream.

Features smaller falls in the background and larger falls in the foreground. All other information is the same as the Forest Fire. $125.00 – 150.00.

"Picture Frame Train" (1953) #LP – 3/PE

The ground moves, wheels turn, headlamp glows, and smoke pours from the stack while houses and trees pass on the left.

Possibly the most vivid of the picture frame series which due to size are more subtle than their larger counterparts. All other information is the same as the Forest Fire. The train featured is the Pioneer Express. $150.00 – 200.00.

"Picture Frame On the Bayou" (1953) #LP – 4/B

Water ripples as the steamboat churns forward, while smoke and fire billow from stacks above and below.

Possibly the most colorful of the picture frame series. All other information is the same as the Forest Fire. $175.00 – 250.00.

"Picture Frame White House" (1953) #LP – 5/WH

Four fountains shoot up and spray downward as water ripples below and in front of them.

The largest fountain actually varies in height, an animation device found in very few other lamps. The stately White House is featured in this lamp, the rarest of the picture frame series. Apparently did not sell well in its own time, a pity since it is a wonderful lamp. All other information is the same as the Forest Fire. $250.00 – 325.00.

"Picture Frame Yellowstone Falls" (1953) #LP-6/YF

Water falls between colorful rocks and moves downstream.

This lamp is harder to find than most of the picture frame series. Features a fine, lush color graphic. All other information is the same as the Forest Fire. $225.00 – 275.00.

"Picture Frame Antique Auto" (1953) #LP-7

The ground moves, wheels spin, and the countryside passes. A flag held by the man on the left in the front seat waves in the wind, and an ascot worn by the lady on the right in the rear sear flaps in the wind.

A lamp that is desirable to old car buffs as well as lamp collectors. The action differs from the standard Econolite antique car lamp. All other information is the same as the Forest Fire. $150.00 – 200.00.

White Christmas (1953) #651

Snow falls on three carolers singing outside a Victorian home.

Rich color and beautiful framing of the scene are highlights of this fine lamp. It is quite delicate, as there is space between the paper scene and the animation glass, making it easily punctured. Christmas collectors will compete to buy it. Very hard to find. $300.00 – 400.00.

"Night Before Christmas" (1953) #652

The logs in the fireplace blaze.

The viewer is looking through a window into a living room decorated for Christmas with children looking on. A charming and lovely graphic, and a lamp that is as fragile in its construction as White Christmas. Even harder to find than its mate. $300.00 – 400.00.

"Hopalong Cassidy – Campfire" (1950)
The campfire burns in the foreground while a waterfall flows in the background.

The front side shows Hoppy talking to an Indian while the rear side has him holding a bandit at gunpoint. The earlier 1949 version has images applied to plastic, making it hard to find intact today as scene flaking was common. The 1950 version uses paper for its scene, usually intact today but sometimes rippled with heat and age. It can be found in red, is much rarer in yellow, and is rarest in light blue. $400.00 – 550.00 depending on color.

Forest Fire (1949) #FF

Fire rages through the trees in the forest.

A lamp from the Roto-Vue, Jr. series, all of which have plastic tops and bottoms with a dark gold color that the company called bronze. There is also a rare red variation that is not as appealing since there is already so much red in the graphic. Not hard to find. $75.00 – 100.00, a bit more for the red model.

Niagara Falls (1950) #NF

Water flows down, churns, and goes downstream.

Another Roto-Vue, Jr. lamp, with excellent falls action that belies its small size. Seen in the television movie *Heart Full of Rain* with Carol Baker and Richard Crenna. Released in the bronze color. Relatively easy to find. $75.00 – 100.00.

Fountain of Youth (1950)

A country boy is peeing into a pond as water swirls on the front side. On the rear side, the explorers stand before the flowing Fountain of Youth.

With a twist of the hand one can choose which side to view. Due to the Roto-Vue, Jr. smaller size and the appealing theme, this lamp was a best seller in its time and still outsells many other lamps. The earliest models had the scene printed on plastic and these are usually flaking badly today. It is advisable to find the later paper scene models that have held up better. The earlier models had a multi-colored foliage outer liner which would hide the side you did not want to show. Models offered even later had only green foliage. Earlier models were released in a rich gold color plastic, while later models were bronze-colored. A very rare red version is sometimes found. $100.00 – 125.00.

72

Fountain of Youth (1950) #861

*A country boy is peeing into a pond as water swirls, and a frog nearby
spews water on the front side. On the rear side the explorers view the
water cascading down the Fountain of Youth.*

The owner has the choice of exposing one side or the other since an outer sleeve with green foliage (often called a "preacher or modesty shade") will allow only one side at a time to be seen. This sleeve is sometimes shrunken with age and may be too tight to turn by hand. Small slits cut in at the bottom may loosen the sleeve, or complete removal may be necessary to see the scene properly. In all of the Fountain of Youth lamps, the stream from the boy actually varies from more to less to a spurt, providing a comic realism that never fails to amuse. This full-sized version was also released in the oval format, but without the added outer sleeve. Harder to find than the Roto-Vue, Jr. model. $125.00 – 150.00.

Why You Should Never Drink Water (1946)

A country boy is peeing into a pond as water swirls, a tiny waterfall flows, and a frog nearby spews water.

This is the first and rarest of the Fountain of Youth lamps. It is winsome since it asks a question on the door of the book framework that has to be opened to see the action and know the answer. It is very delicate, as the paper scene can easily be punctured because there is no support between it and the animation glass. $175.00 – 225.00.

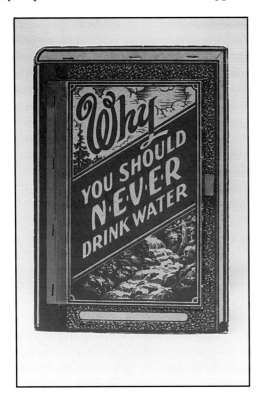

Why You Should Never Drink Water (1949)

Similar to the 1946 model but also 1½" shorter. The question is also printed on the inside of the door which lessens the mystery but is an improvement in the sense that one does not have to open and close the door to understand the joke. Fairly hard to find. $150.00 – 200.00.

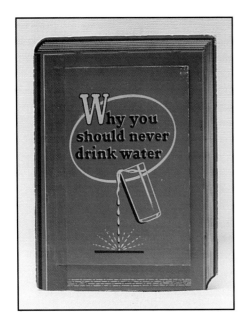

Why You Should Never Drink Water (1954)

Similar to the 1949 model except that the frog is missing and the question appears only on the outside cover. Size-wise, the lamp is comparable to the picture frame series. There is a pull string to open the door, unlike fabric tabs on earlier models that are often missing today. Fairly hard to find. $100.00 – 150.00.

More Here Than Meets The Eye (1952)

*A topless Hawaiian girl in a grass skirt wiggles her hips and her breasts jiggle
while in the background a waterfall flows, and in the foreground a campfire burns.*

A half-door with the words "more here than meets the eye" covers the lower half of the scene and the nudity, so the viewer is greeted by quite a sight upon opening the door. Without a doubt, this is one of the wildest lamps ever produced by Econolite or any other company. The cardboard book framework is surrounded with chrome trim and is loaded with lush and colorful tropical graphics. There is even a seated guitar player who looks like all he is wearing is a lei and his guitar accompanying the girl's dance. The lamp also represents a unique animation attempt never before tried: a moving torso. It is fragile like the Fountain of Youth lamps in that there is no support between the paper scene and the animation glass, so many have a puncture in the paper, often in the corners. Due to its racy nature, it did not sell well in the 1950s, making a great lamp rare today. It is sought after eagerly by lamp collectors and especially by collectors of Hawaiian items. $500.00 – 600.00 and more.

Merry Go Round (1949) #MGR

Children ride animals on a revolving carousel.

This lamp has a carousel litho on an outer plastic sleeve and a colorful paper litho attached to the inner spinning cylinder. An adorable lamp that surfaces less than we would like. It is usually found in red, is rare in yellow, and is rarest in blue. $150.00 – 200.00.

Circus (1952) #401

A parade of circus animals spins by.

This very hard to find Roto-Vue, Jr. children's lamp has colorful circus characters looking up from the bottom and looking out at the top of the outer sleeve. Nicely detailed, it is usually found in red, is rare in yellow, and is rarest in light blue. $175.00 – 225.00.

Totville Train (1948) #B-1
A train with characters moves around the track.

The inner scene of a western town is lit as the plastic train litho (which is affixed to the vented paper top) revolves. An outer small strip of plastic serves as a fence and adds a three-dimensional effect. It is hard to find, and is one of the best of the series called the "Hushabye Lamps" by Econolite. Released in red or in yellow in a version with a stationary top as well as a version with a rotating top (like Mother Goose below). $200.00 – 250.00.

Mother Goose (1948) #C-1 (blue) or #D-1 (pink)
Mother Goose and other nursery rhyme characters spin around.

Words and images appear in full color in one of the most popular of the children's lamps. The inner scene includes Cinderella's castle. The Mother Goose decals are sometimes found deteriorated due to peeling. It was also available in a version with a different construction that has a stationary paper top with no vents and a center opening to allow air flow. In this version, only the Mother Goose graphic moves. Released in blue and in pink. Hard to find in good condition, although it is one of the more common children's lamps. $150.00 – 200.00.

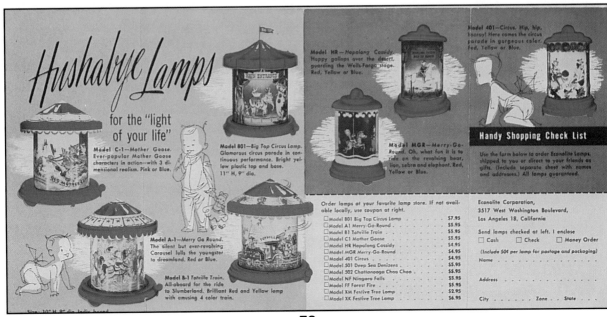

"Mother Goose with Clouds" (1940s)

A lovely variation of the previous model which features a plastic insert with clouds that line the bottom border of the lamp. This gives the unit a special three dimensional feel like the Totville Train. The decals are done in darker colors with different tones and seem to be much less prone to peeling. We have only found this version in pink and it is quite rare. $175.00 – 250.00.

Merry Go Round (1948) #A-1
Children on various animals spin around.

Bright and colorful, this is one of the hardest to find of the carousel style lamps. The paper vents and tabs under the roof are delicate. The inner scene shows a clown, a seal, and a circus master. The paper top is stationary. Released in red. $175.00 – 225.00.

Merry Go Round (1948)
Children on horses spin around.

Hard-to-find carousel framework children's lamp that has an inner scene like model A-1. Paper top is attached to the revolving cylinder. In these Hushabye Lamps, the plastic ball at the end of the switch's pull chain is sometimes completely missing or more often only half of the ball will remain. Released in red and in dark blue which is harder to find. $175.00 – 225.00.

Disneyland (1955)

Disney characters on a carousel or a train revolve.

The lamp made in 1955 to celebrate the newly opened Disneyland. Characters on the bottom tin litho are looking up at the action. A plastic roof sits on the metal framework and is usually missing the center flag and is almost always missing the delicate paper flags supplied with the lamp (that the buyer could glue onto the four metal posts). It was released with a train scene or a carousel scene and was available in red or yellow. Sometimes the posts are natural brass and sometimes they are painted yellow. Desirable crossover collectible. $275.00 – 325.00.

Big Top Circus (1952) #801

Circus figures parade by an opening in the circus tent.

The tent top is yellow plastic and covers a plastic scene shade with a colorful litho graphic that looks like a tent with a ringmaster and clown near the entrance. The rear side shows circus acts. Due to an original price of $7.95 — three dollars more than many of the other Hushabye Lamps — this one is extremely hard to find today. Released in yellow only. $250.00 – 300.00.

Deep Sea Denizens(1952) #501

The shade with boats and fish pictured revolves.

Boats at the top have fishing lines cast into the sea below. An extremely scarce lamp today, probably due to an apparently unpopular simplistic look. Released on a tripod base. $175.00 – 225.00.

Chattanooga Choo Choo (1952) #502

The shade with trains and landscape revolves.

Various trains on trestles, hills, etc., appear on another extremely scarce lamp that also has a simplistic look. Released on a tripod base. Illustration is from the Econolite original sales flyer. $175.00 – 225.00.

"Planter Style Lamps" (1950s)

These lamps featured a standard Econolite round lamp sitting on a structure with ceramic bowls on each side for plants. They stand several inches taller than the regular lamps. Fairly scarce, they usually were released with pleated shades featuring butterfly or fish themes. One either loves or hates these, as they can be unsightly in appearance. Among the tallest standard Econolite lamps at 15½". $175.00 – 250.00.

Old Mill (1961)

Water pours over the paddle wheels and nearby falls pour as water flows downstream.

This strikingly beautiful lamp is arguably an improvement over the earlier Old Mill. It was released only in the oval format and uses the same #765 cylinder as the earlier lamp. Both sides are similar. Extremely hard to find. $350.00 – 400.00.

"Nursery Rhymes" (1953)

A large shade with nursery rhyme characters like Humpty Dumpty, Old King Cole, and 18 others spins around.

The lamp has no wording like some of the other children's lamps. It is decorated simply with characters. With a size and style similar to the Cover Girls lamp, this pedestal base piece is very scarce. Also finding one in good condition is a challenge (as is so with most of the children's lamps) since they were handled quite a bit by little fingers. $150.00 – 200.00.

"Nursery Rhymes Merry Go Round" (1953)

Mother Goose and characters from nursery rhymes spin around.

A very cute little lamp with a pleasing graphic signed by artis Alfred Roarke. It is supported by a pink metal base and used pape construction extensively, making it delicate. The inner scene feature Mary and her garden on a paper sleeve applied over plastic. Ver scarce today. $175.00 – 225.00.

"Our Lady of Guadaloupe" (1953) #R-100

Roses drop from the Madonna's hand into Juan's poncho, halo around her glimmers, and water flows beneath her feet.

Possibly Econolite's first (judging by the number) and onl religious lamp. The scene is based on a Mexican religiou occurrence. It has a worldwide patent notice and a uniqu construction that employs a paper scene behind a plastic win dow, used extensively by Goodman but by Econolite only thi once. It also has a metal weight mounted under the base t prevent tipping, a feature many of us wish had been used mor often. Extremely scarce. $325.00 – 375.00. A vary rare counter part of this lamp, probably foreign-made, is round and features similar graphic and water animation. The most unusual charac teristic is an upper cylinder with an angel graphic that passe under the clouds on the outer sleeve. Value is comparable to it counterpart since rarity balances out the lesser production quality

"One, Two, Buckle My Shoe" (1953)

Building blocks with numbers and other graphics spin around.

Identical in construction to the Nursery Rhymes lamp, although the base color is blue. The paper top includes graphics of kids in various poses with corresponding captions to illustrate the well-known nursery rhyme. Very scarce. $175.00 – 225.00.

84

Christmas Trees/Santa Claus Lamps (1948 – 1952)

Colored light glows through openings in the trees as they revolve.

Econolite's line of Christmas trees was popular then and now. They are delicate since they are entirely paper with a metal support band running around the bottom. They are enhanced with glitter and have openings cut-in all around for air flow. They pivot on a metal shaft mounted to a plastic base. More often than not they are found in their original boxes, as they were usually stored that way from one year to the next. All boxes included paper cones for shade support and cardboard pads for protection. If you are lucky, you may still find in the box a tiny paper card containing a paper star that could be punched out and put on the tree top. The most common size is the smallest and is 10½" in height (model XM). The next size is rarer and stands 15" tall (model X). The 15" size was also released in all colors in a version with more pronounced white highlights. The largest and rarest is the 23" tree (model XK). All sizes were released in white, red, green, and blue, with the last two colors being harder to find. The trees were also released in a much rarer gold and white, and in a rare and lovely Noel graphics model (XN). Both of these were available only in the 15" size. The finest release was probably the Santa Claus lamp that featured a nicely drawn Santa on both sides (XMS, XS, and XKS). This one is also quite hard to find. The small trees came with 25-watt bulbs, the medium trees with 60-watt bulbs, and the large trees with 100-watt bulbs. The bulb color always matched the shade color, or you could order a different color for 40 to 75 cents more. In the original instructions, Econolite specified that the white trees required blue bulbs and to get the maximum sparkle from the trees, they should be used in well-lit rooms. You might also try using white bulbs which give a very nice look. Originally, the smallest tree was priced at $2.95, while the largest went for $6.95 which accounts for their relative scarcity today. 10½", $75.00 – 100.00; 15", $125.00 – 150.00; 23", $150.00 – 200.00. Add $50.00 or more for Santa versions. (See More Motion Sickness chapter for two 15" variations.)

"Auto Insurance" (1950s)

An overturned car blazes while a fire extinguisher sprays and a "Think" sign flashes.

This is an Econolite Motion-in-Advertising display. It is made of heavy cardboard with a construction style in the rear very much like the picture frame lamps. This is a large display unit that could have appeared in an insurance agency office to attract attention. It looks rather comical when one considers how that tiny fire extinguisher could put out such a huge fire! Since these lamps were not sold to the general public, they are very scarce and valued advertising collectibles. $450.00 – 550.00.

"You Can't Live In The Ruins" (1950)

A house blazes while water from hoses pumps out.

Another Motion-in-Advertising insurance specialty lamp. Like the auto insurance display, the construction features an outer framework of graphics that sits a couple of inches out from the animation area and gives a three-dimensional look to the piece. $400.00 – 500.00.

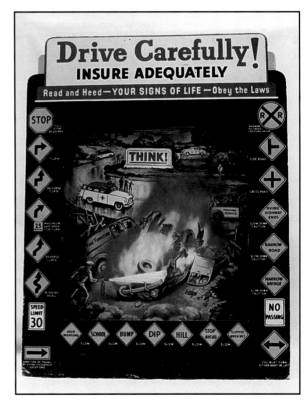

"Prevent Forest Fires" (1950s)

Fire blazes and the river flows.

Another Motion-in-Advertising display with a three-dimensional design. The label on the back reads "Scene-in-Action unit," a name they employed regularly on these specialty lamps. Messages reading "prevent forest and range fires, grow more trees, and keep America green" well amplify the point of the animation. A nice size for home collections. $350.00 – 400.00.

"Rainier Beer" (1940s)

Water falls.

This large unit features two bulbs, one for general lighting and one for turning the cylinder. Attractive and scarce. $250.00 – 300.00.

"Coor's Beer Display" (1940s)

Water falls.

Sizeable unit with a glass front that would promote the product. Scarce. $200.00 – 250.00.

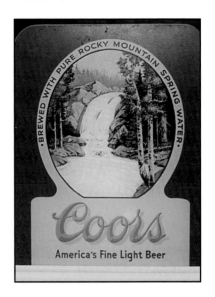

"U & I Sugar" (1940s)

Sugar pours while liquid below bubbles and product words are highlighted.

Sizable specialty lamp with a seldom found theme, that of sugar pouring. This example is missing the sugar bag graphic on the left. $350.00 – 400.00.

"Disney Lamp" (1950s)

This is not a motion lamp but is included as an interesting piece since it is marked "Manufactured and Distributed by Econolite Corp." The drum-shaped base with Mickey and other characters was supplied with a matching paper shade. It was probably sold around the time Disneyland first opened. Scarce. A matching lamp was released in blue with different graphics. Possibly one was for boys and the other for girls. $150.00 – 225.00 with shade.

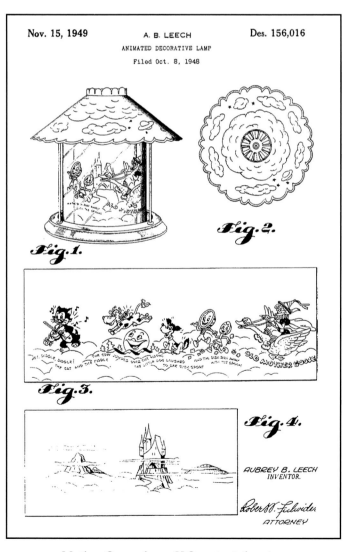

Mother Goose lamp U.S. patent drawing.

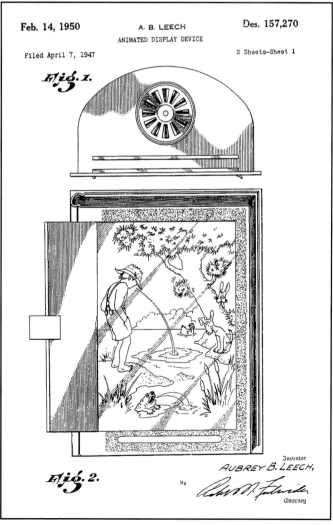

Why You Should Never Drink Water lamp U.S. patent drawing.

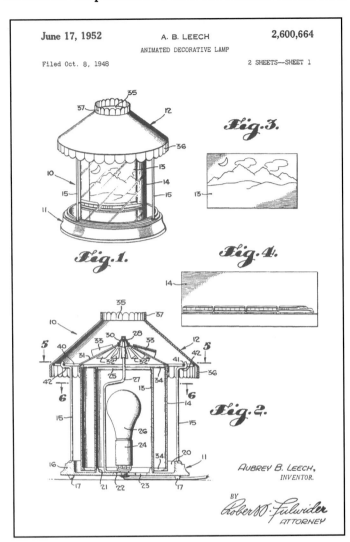

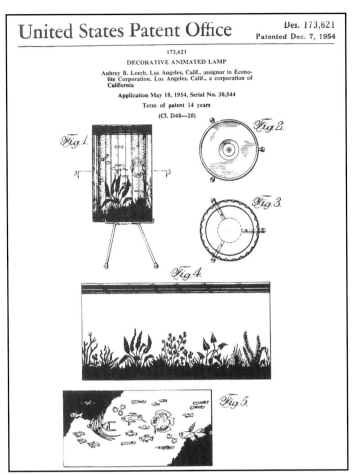

June 17, 1952   A. B. LEECH   2,600,664

ANIMATED DECORATIVE LAMP

Filed Oct. 8, 1948   2 SHEETS—SHEET 1

AUBREY B. LEECH,
INVENTOR.

BY Robert O. Fulwider
ATTORNEY

United States Patent Office

Des. 173,621
Patented Dec. 7, 1954

173,621

DECORATIVE ANIMATED LAMP

Aubrey B. Leech, Los Angeles, Calif., assignor to Econolite Corporation, Los Angeles, Calif., a corporation of
California

Application May 18, 1954, Serial No. 30,544

Term of patent 14 years

(Cl. D48—20)

U.S. patent drawings.

U.S. patent drawings.

Econolite's ANIMATED GIFT LAMPS

turn LIGHT sales

into HEAVY PROFITS

for Home, Office Store, Hotel, Restaurant

MODEL 953 **mallards in flight**

A no-limit seller, with millions of nature lovers as prospective purchasers. Fibre-Glo shade presents realistic illusion of game birds in full flight. Fascinating and restful to watch. 6¾" Diameter, 14" High— with wrought iron tripod legs. Bulb included.

MODEL X **festive lamp**

Econolite's famous "special occasion" holiday lamp, with cone shaped parchment type shade in Blue, Red, Green or White. Covered with mirrored, highly polished aluminum and glass "flitter"...tarnish proof! Polystyrene base. 16½" High, 9" Diameter. Bulb included.

ECONOLITE CORPORATION 3517 W. Washington Blvd., Los Angeles 18, Calif.

CREATORS OF ANIMATED FESTIVE LAMPS, TV LAMPS, SCENIC NOVELTY
LAMPS, HUSHABYE LAMPS, GLAMOUR TOYS, BOUNCEY PLAY BALLS

Ad from *Gift and Art Buyers Annual,* 1955 – 56.

L.A. Goodman Manufacturing Company

Based in Chicago, Illinois, Goodman started production in the mid-1950s and continued until about 1972. They called their animated lamps "roto-action scenic lamps." Their corporate name changed from L.A. Goodman to Lagco to Lacolite along the way. The Lacolite office was located at 936 North Michigan Ave., while the factory was at 131 W. 63rd St. The company started using brass-plated bases similar to Econolite and later began using colored plastic bases. The earliest metal bases had a small round hole pattern, followed by a pattern using three levels of x's, and the last and most common pattern used squares. Plastic bases were yellow, sometimes white, and incorporated power switches into the line cord. Goodman also sometimes downgraded quality from the earlier rich color models to later models with flat one-tone colors. The lighthouse lamp is a good example of this regression. Earliest models often had litho work on outside surfaces of the shade and have held up quite well. They may be identified by a satin finish and usually do not have a white border at the very top. Later, inside surface litho models may be subject to scene flaking. Often the eye cannot detect this deterioration unless a lamp is lit, so the rule of thumb is always light up a Goodman lamp with this type of construction before buying and avoid disappointment. At flea markets especially, where electricity is hard to find, do try to find a place to light such a lamp.

Old L.A. Goodman factory as seen today at 131 W. 63rd. St. Note the Lacolite name still on building.

Many Goodman lamps show great thematic similarity to concurrent Econolite lamps. Some of the butterfly and fish lamps are choice examples. Generally their litho quality is not as fine, but by all means do not avoid searching for Goodman lamps since there are plenty of rewarding finds. The Firefighters lamp is as good a find as many of the better Econolites. Remember, too, that Goodman was fairly prolific in the motion lamp field, producing over 50 models that we can document. Their wide oval

This shows how a badly flaked Goodman shade looks when lit.

lamps are gems, due to a full 7½" to 8½" panoramic scene area. And these were not "squeezed" versions of the regular round lamps. The wide oval lamps were designed independently and most were released in 1959, several years after their round counterparts. That late date makes them a good bit harder to find than the round ones. Their picture areas are bordered with gold (that tends to flake) and they are only one-sided, but they are quite special to collect.

Standard Goodman lamps stand 11½" tall, while the wide ovals are 11", the bowl-shaped lamps are 10", and pedestal models are tallest at 14". Take note that many Goodman lamps look more vivid unlit than Econolite lamps do when they are not lit. Goodman lamps' shiny plastic surfaces account for this difference. Econolite lamps have a satin finish that makes them look somewhat dull when off.

Dating Goodman lamps is fairly easy since most included a date in fine white print on the cardboard lamp tops, or in lower border areas. Their animation sleeves and cylinders were usually not identified as well as Econolite products.

We could criticize Goodman lamps by pointing to the over-usage of the pleated shade style to create "distortion" animation for about half of their output. The effects created, while colorful and pleasant, are far less captivating than lamps using true animation. Some examples using pleated shades are downright silly; look at the Davy Crockett lamp. However, the fact that Goodman and Econolite were competitive over such a long and similar time frame surely added to the quality and number of lamps produced by both. What collector today will complain about that?

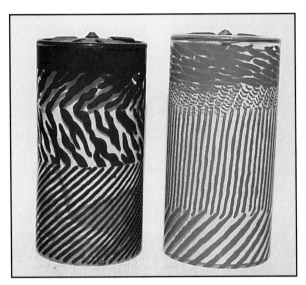

A note about Goodman cylinders: Late in production, probably in the late 1960s, the company decided to use the "wrong" cylinders in some of their lamps. We don't know if they used existing stock for convenience or if it was easier to use one cylinder for several lamps, but many cylinders do not match in later lamps. The Racing Trains, for instance, used an upside down Niagara Falls cylinder for animation. The effect is close, but not as good as an original train cylinder would be. For their Forest Fire, they later used an upside down Waterfall-Campfire cylinder, which yields a less ferocious blaze to the fire. If you have a lamp like one of these, try to look for an earlier, correct cylinder to improve your animation.

An original Goodman train cylinder on the left and a later replacement train cylinder on the right.

Forest Fire – Wildlife (1956) #2003
Fire blazes in the trees, while water flows downstream.

This is a very popular lamp. The front side includes animals in a stream while the rear includes a cabin. Rich red colors add to its effectiveness. Released in round and wide oval formats. Water flows in the opposite direction in the wide lamp. $100.00 – 125.00.

Niagara Falls (1957) #2007

Water flows down, churns at bottom, and flows downstream.

One of the most common Goodman lamps and one of the most common Niagara Falls lamps. The water action is not as realistic as an Econolite but is still impressive due to the bold graphic and a broad water flow style. Released in round and wide oval formats. One variation, sold at the famous landmark, says "Souvenir of Niagara Falls" in gold lettering on the black cardboard top along with a gold shield with a star inside on the left and a gold maple leaf on the right. The lamp is also titled in bold black letters at upper front side. Still another variation finds the same lamp enclosed with a solid brass base and brass top. Easy to find. $100.00 – 125.00. Variations $125.00 – 175.00.

Waterfall – Campfire (1956)

Water falls down a steep drop, moves to the right,
moves down again, and then flows downstream on the
front side. The rear side features a campfire that flickers.

Without a doubt, the setting must be Yellowstone Falls. This is an attractive lamp with glowing red rocks giving a colorful effect. The rear side has probably the dullest animation on any lamp. Take note of the lack of a white border at the very top of the lamp. This is an example of an earlier outside printed shade. Also, an unusual specimen is shown that has the water flowing to the left. Released in round and wide oval formats. Fairly common. $100.00 – 150.00. Add $50.00 for wide oval.

Lighthouse (1956)

Waves spill over the shore and crash over the lighthouse while water churns and the lighthouse beacon flashes on the front side. Clouds also change color in earlier models. The rear shows a sailing vessel and has waves rippling underneath.

This is an extremely popular lamp and relatively easy to locate. Released in round and wide oval formats. $125.00 – 175.00. Add $50.00 for wide oval.

Firefighters (1957)

The ground moves under the horses, firemen, and fire engine while dust is churned by the horses' hooves. Fire and smoke billow out of the stack, and jets of water pump out of the hoses and hit the blazing fire.

One of the best Goodman creations, loaded with animation and color. The front shows the firefighters while the rear shows the antique fire engine. You will have trouble deciding which side to favor! Released in round and wide oval formats, but note that the oval style curiously leaves out the ground moving effects! Also, the round release was printed in two distinctly different colorations. Rather scarce. $300.00 – 350.00. Add $50.00 for wide oval.

Oriental Fantasy (1957)

Water ripples and flows while a volcano erupts at intervals.

A lamp which features an unusual yellow color and a fascinating, intermittent eruption of the volcano on the front side. The rear side is similar but lacks the volcano. Intermittent action (carried out by cylinder design) is rarely found on motion lamps, so this is a stand-out, along with much better than average graphics. Released in the round format. Moderately scarce. $200.00 – 250.00.

Trains Racing (1957)

The ground moves, wheels spin, smoke and fire billow out of stacks, and whistles steam, while head-lamps glow.

A nice, vivid lamp but not quite as realistic as the Econolite Trains. Interesting in that it shows three different trains racing together. Released in round and wide oval formats although extremely scarce in oval. Relatively common in the round format. $150.00 – 200.00. Add $50.00 for wide oval.

"Ships Burning" (1958)

Fire blazes on ships after a battle, and water ripples while wood fragments sizzle.

A bold and striking lamp which is a top choice among Goodman creations. Why their common forest fire would outsell this stunning ship fire by probably 50 to one is beyond imagination. Released in the round format. Quite scarce. $300.00 – 350.00

Birches (1956)

Water ripples and flows while clouds shift and change colors.

This is one of the most beautiful Goodman lamps, designed to be viewed on one side only. It is constructed with a plastic litho scene affixed to the inside of the plastic window. The rear has a white and gold fleck design pattern. Gold borders frame the window area and the top perimeters, and today the delicate gold is often flaking. There are four lamps in this series. They feature better than average color since the litho process was applied to both sides of the scene panel. Released in the round format. Relatively hard to find. $225.00 – 275.00.

"Birches With Duck" (1956)

Water ripples and flows.

This lamp is the second in a series and is similar to Birches graphically although a bit less interesting. Still, it is a beauty. Released in the round format. Relatively hard to find. $225.00 – 275.00.

"Autumn" (1956)

Clouds drift by and change colors while wind rustles above and below the trees.

This features a beautiful country setting. It looks pretty even when off. This lamp is third in a series. Released in the round format. Very scarce. $250.00 – 300.00.

"Farmhouse" (1956)

Clouds shift and change colors while wind rustles the trees.

The animation tries hard to achieve a motion that is difficult to accomplish, and here is not totally successful. However, the scene is pretty, and this is absolutely the rarest of the four in the series. Note that the cylinder inside says "WT-AUTUMN" on it. Released in the round format. $250.00 – 325.00.

Ocean Creatures (1955)

An octopus, fish, and other undersea creatures swim by.

The pleated inner sleeve creates the motion effects. The outer plastic sleeve is printed with undersea foliage in gold. Cylinder images cannot be seen when the lamp is off, a trait common to all pleated shade lamps. Released in the round format. Fairly scarce. $200.00 – 250.00.

"Ocean Creatures By Sunken Ship" (1955)

An octopus, fish, and other undersea creatures swim by.

This lamp is identical to Ocean Creatures except that the outer sleeve is printed with a sunken ship and treasure chest theme. Released in the round format on a pedestal base. An unusual variation was found with factory-made round air holes surrounding the typical large center air hole on the top. Scarce. $250.00 – 300.00.

Sailboats (1954)

Colorful sailboats pass by and water ripples below.

The inner pleated sleeve creates the motion effects. The outer sleeve is printed with trees and foliage by the shoreline. Released in the round format on a pedestal base. Some shades feature tighter and more numerous pleats for somewhat better animation. Also released on standard base with gold foliage theme identical to that found on Butterflies and Flowers lamp (p. 102). Fairly scarce. $225.00 – 275.00.

Flying Geese (1957)

Geese fly by as water ripples below and clouds shift above.

The pleated inner sleeve creates the motion effects. The outer plastic sleeve is printed with gold foliage. The colorful birds make a pleasing sight. Released in the round format on regular and pedestal bases. Here is a real piece of trivia: nearly all Goodman and Econolite standard lamps have brown-colored power switch knobs, but the base shown sports a white-colored (and very good looking) power switch knob. Also released with a shade featuring spade-like patterns on top and bottom borders and tighter and more numerous pleats. Not too hard to find. $150.00 – 200.00.

"Flames" (1954?)

Colored flames rise.

This is a very strange lamp in that it only shows flames burning in mid-air. It uses a pleated inner sleeve for the motion effects. Very scarce and can appear on a regular or pedestal base in the round format. $100.00 – 150.00.

"Butterflies and Flowers" (1956)

Butterflies flutter by as flowers below wave in the wind.

Another pleated sleeve lamp which creates action that is pleasing for the butterflies but a bit phony for the flowers. It is very colorful and the outer shade is printed with foliage in gold. Released in the round format on regular and pedestal bases. Somewhat scarce. $200.00 – 250.00.

"Dancing Nymphs" (1957)

Nude young ladies in silhouette cavort and dance by.

The pleated inner sleeve allows the ladies to appear as if they are dancing. It is not exactly provocative but is certainly appealing and very scarce. Released in the round format. $250.00 – 300.00.

Santa and the Reindeer (1955)

Santa, his sleigh and all the reindeer fly over Victorian rooftops.

The beautiful colors on the cylinder revolving against stark black silhouettes of homes below combine to make a very fine lamp. It is desirable, a crossover collectible, and quite scarce. It uses a pleated inner shade for motion and was released on the pedestal base in the round format. $400.00 – 500.00.

Davy Crockett (1955)

Davy, some Indians, and a bear spin by.

Another pleated sleeve lamp with bold cylinder colors. The outer sleeve has black and cream-colored foliage along with the name "Davy Crockett." We feel the action is somewhat silly since the animated figures look static. The wavy effect doesn't quite work with them as it does with butterflies or fish. However, this lamp is still very desirable, loaded with color, and a crossover collectible. Released on a pedestal base in the round format. Very scarce. $400.00 – 550.00.

"Plantation Scene" (1957)

Carriages and southern belles and gentlemen pass by.

The scene could be right out of "Gone With the Wind" with the period dress and style. Warm colors on the inner cylinder project onto the pleated sleeve with an outer sleeve imprinted with foliage in black. Fairly scarce and released in the round format. $200.00 – 250.00.

"Florida Scene" (1957)

Palm trees, a tiny island, a tiny sailboat, and more spin by in color.

Another pleated sleeve animated lamp with effects and a look similar to the Plantation Scene. Released in the round format and very scarce. $200.00 – 250.00.

"Peacocks" (1955)

Two peacocks pass by; one has feathers up, the other has feathers down.

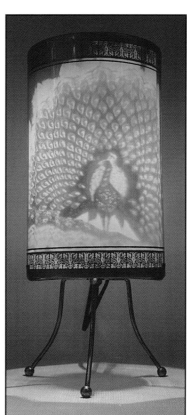

The lamp is "pretty as a peacock" with its rainbow of colors, but has a rather silly action with the wavy effect given by the pleated sleeve. Released in the round format on a gold pedestal base with rather unusual curved legs. It can be found with a gold pattern imprinted shade or a black pattern one. Very scarce. $225.00 – 275.00.

"Planets" (1957)
Colorful planets revolve.

Once again, the pleated sleeve creates a strange action since the planets look wavy as they pass. The outer sleeve has a solar theme imprinted on the bottom. Released in the round format and very scarce. $250.00 – 300.00.

"Flying Geese in Bowl" (1957)
Geese fly by as water ripples below and clouds shift above.

This is one of several unique bowl-shaped designs used by Goodman. The pleated sides of the bowl create the animation effects. The lamp tops at this age are very brittle and can fall off easily since they are not attached. The structure is imprinted with gold foliage over either white or blue background colors. Scarce. $200.00 – 250.00.

"Fish in Bowl" (1957)
Tropical fish swim by.

The graphic even includes a shark and a turtle! Similar to Flying Geese above; the same comments apply. You might use a matching colored plastic dish with a hole cut out of the center if the original top is gone. $225.00 – 275.00.

"Butterflies and Flowers in Bowl" (1957)

Butterflies flutter by and flowers below wave in the wind.

Similar to Flying Geese on previous pages; the same comments apply. $200.00 – 250.00.

"Flowers in Bowl" (1957)

Flowers wave in the wind.

The flowers in this graphic are larger than those found with the butterflies. Similar to Flying Geese and its descriptions. The action is less realistic on this model, but it is the hardest to find of the group. $225.00 – 275.00.

Fish in the Windows (1957)

Colorful fish swim by.

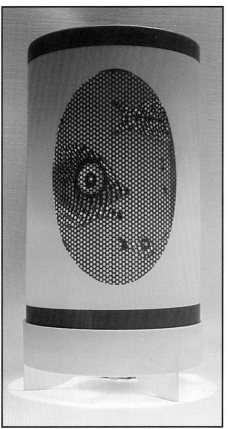

Oval windows on the outer shade have a dot pattern litho imprinted which creates an unusual type of distortion animation that allows the figures to glisten as well as to appear to be moving. The animation has a decidedly modern, offbeat look. Released in the round format on a plastic base. Very scarce. $175.00 – 225.00.

"Teddy Bears on Bicycles" (1957?)

Cute teddy bears ride by on their bikes.

Very similar to Fish in the Windows in design and animation but with a blue rather than green outer sleeve color. Very scarce. $175.00 – 225.00.

"Merry Christmas" (1970s)

The outlines of the figures and words glimmer.

This is a very late lamp using the Lacolite name. Cartoon-like images make it inferior to Santa and the Reindeer of the 1950s. Still, it is a worthy lamp, a crossover collectible, and somewhat scarce. Released in the round format on a plastic base. $125.00 – 175.00.

"Niagara Falls" (1970s)

Water falls and flows downstream.

A lamp that is novel since it uses an actual photograph of the falls for its graphic. Possibly made in Canada, it has construction similarities to Lacolite products and we have therefore placed it in this grouping. It shows relatively unrealistic animation. Released in the round format and fairly scarce. $100.00 – 125.00.

Storybook (1957)

Humpty Dumpty, Little Bo Peep, and other characters whirl around while highlights and stars sparkle.

This is one very colorful lamp that uses a striped plastic sleeve around the bulb to create the sparkle effects. The outside sleeve contains a litho of a boy, a girl, and a dog in a playroom setting. It offers a very pleasing and captivating look. Released in the round format and very scarce. $250.00 – 300.00.

"Circus" (1950s)

Halos around circus figures glisten as the shade spins around.

This children's lamp is lively and has a center core of striped, colored bars which interacts with holes punched in the outer revolving shade to create its motion effects. Released on a metal base and very scarce. $175.00 – 225.00.

"Western Scene" (1950s)

This lamp is similar to the Circus lamp but has Western figures instead.

The base shown is probably not original. It is interesting that the design of this lamp allowed it to be placed on just about any standard non-motion lamp base. $175.00 – 225.00 with original base.

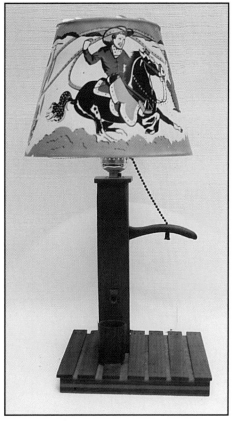

107

Mistress Mary (1957)

A square shade with nursery rhyme characters spins around.

This is one of the Goodman Juvenile Rotary Lamp series. Certainly out of the ordinary, the shade is embossed on this rather small lamp. Characters are Mary Quite Contrary, Little Bo Peep, Little Miss Muffet, and Mother Goose. Fairly scarce. $100.00 – 150.00.

"Master Jack" (1957)

Exactly like the lamp at left except it features all male characters, Little Jack Horner, Little Boy Blue, Humpty Dumpty, and Jack Be Nimble. We recently found an example of this lamp with one male and three female characters. Even scarcer. $125.00 – 175.00.

"Bathing Beauties" (1950s)

A square shade with girls in bathing suits spins around.

An embossed shade like Mistress Mary but with an adult theme, as shapely women add to its appeal. Very scarce. $175.00 – 225.00.

"Fountain of Youth" (1950s?)

A country boy pees into a pond which ripples as a nearby dog watches.

Its action is not as realistic as an Econolite Fountain of Youth, but its graphics are quite colorful and appealing. Released in the round format and very scarce. Possibly a case where Econolite's successful marketing of this theme inspired Goodman to follow in their footsteps. $150.00 – 175.00.

"Winter Scene" (1970s)
Snow glistens.

This is a very late release by Lacolite. It is not at all realistic, but they might have been aiming for a contemporary look. Released in the round format and hard to find. $150.00 – 200.00.

"Table Lamp with Waterfall – Campfire" (1950s)

Action is the same as Waterfall–Campfire lamp. This is a unique lamp structure, featuring metal framework surrounding a regular round motion lamp. A three-way switch allows turning on the bulb at top, the motion unit below, or both simultaneously. It was also released with the Lighthouse motif and may exist in other variations. Note that the lampshade and the finial are not original. Very scarce. $200.00 – 250.00.

"Christmas Tree"
The bulb glows through openings in the tree as it revolves.

While Econolite used paper for their Christmas trees, Goodman used plastic, so they are in generally better shape today. They stood 15" tall and featured details of garland, ornaments, and more. Released in a green basic color and in a pink basic color. A recently found blue example shows a winter setting with the words "Season's Greetings." (See More Motion Sickness chapter for a variation.) Very scarce. $150.00 – 200.00.

Sparkelite Christmas Tree (1950s) #97

Christmas tree sparkles as it revolves.

Using the same tree as at the end of the previous page, Goodman added an inner striped cone-shaped cylinder of red, white, and blue to give a strobe-like sparkle effect that is eye catching. As far as we know, all Goodman Christmas trees were supplied with a green plastic base and have a non-pointed top where possibly a star or ornament was placed. Air holes for this style are found only on the top third. Also released in green. Extremely scarce. $175.00 – 250.00.

"Barber Shop Pole" (1950s)

Color striped barber pole and the words "you are next" revolve.

This is an unusual Lagco release with a metal shade top that can hold advertising information on small clips supplied. The words "novelty rotary lamp" appear under the base. Extremely scarce as it was not sold to the general public. $200.00 – 250.00.

"Pfeiffer's Beer" (1950s)

The product name changes color while words and musical notes travel by and out of the mouth of the fife player.

Goodman created a line of advertising display pieces they called "3-D Displays" and this is one of the most attractive. It features extruded images in plastic with cardboard construction in the rear. Quite scarce as it was not sold to the general public. $200.00 – 250.00.

"American Beer" (1950s)

Wheat rustles in the wind as clouds pass by.

This is a Goodman advertising lamp that uses an amazingly different effect of wheat waving in the wind. It is constructed of cardboard, paper, and plastic. The scene is easily punctured, having no support behind it. This is unusual since most Goodman advertising pieces were of the three dimensional variety. Quite scarce. $225.00 – 275.00.

"National Bohemian Beer" (1950s)

Beer pours from a tap into a mug.

Another 3-D Display, this lamp is colorful and attractive. Quite scarce. These commercial displays were identified only by a seal that was pasted on and is sometimes missing. $200.00 – 250.00.

"Sir John Schenley Whisky" (1950s)

Words project and move past the globe of the world.

The extruded plastic images produce a pleasing display, and the plastic product bottle stands out. Very likely one of the Goodman 3-D Displays so it is included here. $200.00 – 250.00.

"Erin Beer" (1950s)

The shade revolves.

A Lagco Novelty Rotary Lamp whose molded plastic shade features two panels with a bottle of Erin beer and two opposing panels with the product label. Erin beer was made by Standard Brewing Company of Cleveland, Ohio. The same shape and style as the standard release Mistress Mary lamp. The identical style was also used for a lamp featuring American Beer. Very scarce. $125.00 – 150.00.

five easy steps to set up your new Lamp

Your new Roto-Action Lamp will provide years of enjoyment if these simple points are followed carefully...

1 Place Roto-Lamp base on any level surface and remove protective cork from point on upright pivot wire.

Roto-Action Lamps are designed for use with regular 60 watt clear or frosted bulbs--do not use larger bulbs as their greater heat may cause damage.

2 Balance inner cylinder on point of pivot wire so that jewel bearing in the center of smaller cylinder rests exactly on pivot point.

If you desire to speed up the Roto-Action, merely open the "fan blades" a little wider on the top of the inner cylinder. Closing the blades slightly will slow the action.

3 Place the lamp shade down over the inner cylinder so that it rests securely on the base of the lamp. Be careful not to jar the inner cylinder so that the bearing comes off the pivot point.

IMPORTANT NOTE:

On rare occasions, the first time your lamp is turned on, it may not rotate, or it may rotate in reverse. This is caused by harmless static build-up. To make this static go away and "unstick" the cylinder so it will rotate, simply use the enclosed towelette and wipe inside surface of the lamp shade, and both inside and outside surfaces of the inner cylinder. – DO NOT WIPE DRY – because this can cause static again. Now your lamp should rotate freely each time it is switched on.

4 Gently spin the inner cylinder to make certain it rotates freely without touching the shade. If touching does occur, either the base is not on a level surface or the pivot wire is not upright enough. You can easily adjust the pivot wire to a more perfect straight and upright position by bending it slightly.

5 Now, turn on the switch and the inner cylinder should start to rotate as the heat from the light bulb rises up through the "fan blades" in the top of the inner cylinder--producing a fascinating Roto-Action effect.

LACOLITE INDUSTRIES
DIVISION OF HOUSEWARES, INC.

OFFICE
936 North Michigan Avenue
Chicago, Illinois 60611

FACTORY
131 West 63rd Street
Chicago, Illinois 60621

Original instructions for assembling an L.A. Goodman lamp.

"Santa Claus at North Pole" (1950s)

This is not a motion lamp but is included as an interesting Goodman release in that it has the familiar but narrower metal base and a plastic shade with colorful graphics. All it does is light up. How tempted we are to turn it into a snow falling lamp! Scarce. $50.00 – 75.00.

112

❦ European Lamp Producers ❧

The bulk of this chapter was written from notes and information provided by Lieutenant Colonel Fred T. Pribble. Fred was stationed in Germany from 1995 to 1997. During that time he aggressively sought out and purchased motion lamps from private collectors, flea markets, and antique shows. He managed to find over 40 different lamps and 20 duplicates, an impressive yield for a hard-to-find commodity in a fairly short time period. He discovered that in Europe a sort of parallel universe of motion lamps existed that mirrored some of the activity that took place in the United States with some lamps and manufacturers. Rather than finding the older lamps from the 1920s to the 1940s as expected, he found lamps mostly from the 1950s to the 1970s. The Econolite Corporation has been the predominant influence in Europe, as over two-thirds of his finds were lamps manufactured by Econolite, lamps manufactured under license from Econolite, or inferior European manufactured imitations of Econolite lamps. The lamps in the latter category seemed to "reverse engineer" or closely knock off Econolite designs. Only one lamp found had been copied from an L. A. Goodman original, and some lamps are clearly original European motifs, but there were very few of these. Interestingly, some of what is common here seems to be scarce in Europe, like the Niagara Falls lamp. However, a fairly common lamp like the Old Mill is fairly abundant in Europe, possibly due to the European love of nature and the outdoors. Not surprisingly, lamps of European landmarks are much easier to find overseas. Fred found three Eiffel Tower lamps there, while we have seen only one in our travels here. In fact, he feels that these lamps and others showing European locales (Venice Canal, Fountains of Rome, Fountains of Versailles, etc.) were developed to target the European market and therefore are much more abundant there than in this country. While many Econolite lamps that surfaced were originally sold in military Post Exchanges (PXs) and were supplied with 220-volt bulbs and plug adapters, others were sold in local stores. Fred has attempted to categorize and identify the lamps by piecing together what little printed information could be found and by talking to people there. Since only two manufacturers actually labeled their lamps, much of the process has been educated guesswork. Anna and I have only found three or four European lamps for sale in this country, but many were probably brought back by servicemen or shipped here by other people. With the Internet and the Web bringing the world together more and more, we feel exposure to European lamps and their special beauty will assist collectors in seeking out more of these fine pieces. Read on and enjoy, but keep in mind that most of the following lamps will be hard to find. Note that these descriptions do not include the motion of any lamp that was covered previously in the book.

"Gold Topped" Econolite Lamps

The single trait that each lamp in this category has in common is its distinctive gold top, hence the name. The top is textured cardboard found on many later and oval Econolite lamps here and abroad. The quality of the lithography, silk screening on both sides of the outer shade surface, and, in particular, the vivid colors strongly suggest that the lamps were made under license from the Econolite Corporation.

It is important to note, however, that while the outer shades are similar, they are not always identical to the original Econolite lamps. Moreover, the animation sleeves and cylinders are often different in design and color from the original Econolite version, often producing decidedly different results. The cylinders were joined with a vertical seam rather than a diagonal one which sometimes causes a visible line when a lamp is lit. In some lamps the degree of realism found in the American version is somewhat lacking in the European example while the degree of color saturation in the European lamp is often superior. Two good examples of this are the Fountains of Versailles and the Eiffel Tower lamps. The American versions of these lamps are more realistic with skies and clouds in particular having more detail. On the other hand, the European examples are much more colorful, and the colors used are deeper and richer. Generally speaking, the animation on European lamps is less vivid than on similar American versions, mostly due to animation sleeve and cylinder differences.

Gold topped Econolites are also distinguishable from their American cousins by their bases. It appears that the earlier lamps used a carved wood base while later models used a uniquely designed chrome-plated base with black plastic balls for feet. In addition, virtually all the lamps were manufactured in the oval shape. Oddly, the production and model numbering system used by the Econolite Corporation is not normally present on these lamps. The pivot rod arm on these lamps has a metal sleeve attached at the top with a separate detachable point. There are two screws on the sleeve; one affixes the sleeve to the pivot rod arm, the other holds the point in place. This innovation allows for the point to be raised or lowered to achieve better alignment between the cylinder and the animation sleeve.

Unfortunately, none of the lamps bear any type of identification about the manufacturer or the country of origin. The outer shade does, however, bear the original Econolite copyright date which also supports the assumption that they were made under license. Fortunately, scrap metal was used to form the fans of the cylinders, in particular old beer and oil cans. The language on the underside of these fans seems to be Dutch. Accordingly, it is possible that the lamps were made somewhere in the Netherlands.

"Fish" (1954)

The cylinder graphics are very similar to the American version. The pleated inner shade is plastic rather than paper so the pleats are whiter and less problematic. The base is round and wooden. Scarce. $200.00 – 250.00.

"Fountains of Versailles" (1963)

One of the last releases of the Econolite Corporation and one repeated on the European market depicting the opulent palace and grounds of Louis XIV, the Sun King. The rear side, which features Apollo in his chariot riding toward the sun surrounded by four Tritons, is misspelled "Apoll's Basin" just like the American version. Uses a blue colored cylinder (remember that most American cylinders are white) and this cylinder is the same one found in Eiffel Tower, Niagara Falls, and Old Mill lamps shown following. The base is silver metal, but note that the balls used are silver in color and not black. Very scarce. $400.00 – 450.00.

"Eiffel Tower" (1963)

An absolutely beautiful lamp. The Place de la Concorde on the rear is the spot where Louis the XVI, Marie Antoinette, and Robespierre lost their heads, and we are sure some of you will also lose your heads attempting to secure this lamp! Also depicted is the Egyptian obelisk from Luxor, the oldest man-made object in Paris. The graphic details are superb, right down to the individual cobblestones. Very desirable and very scarce. $475.00 – 550.00.

"Forest Fire" (1955)

A faithful rendering of the American version. A somewhat different cylinder is used in this one. Again, a wooden base that is nicely carved and stained. Easier to find than some. $125.00 – 150.00.

115

"Niagara Falls" (1955)

The animation sleeve is colored blue, and with the blue cylinder spinning, the net effect is a very deep and dark blue hue to the whole scene when lit, making it very distinctive from the U.S. version. Scarce. $150.00 – 200.00.

"Old Mill" (1956)

This particular lamp, while bearing the signature "gold top," has a decidedly different look. The outer shade surface is shiny plastic so it has the look of an L.A. Goodman lamp more than an Econolite. There is no Econolite copyright marking. The base is brown plastic and is virtually identical to the bases under the A. Leuchten Company described beginning on page 119. Released in round as well as oval formats. Scarce. $175.00 – 200.00.

"Antique Car" (1957)

The lithographic color and quality are somewhat superior to the American version, especially as to vivid reds and oranges. Very desirable and very scarce. $225.00 – 275.00.

"Hearth" (1958)

Excellent graphics and motion effects. Tends to be heavier on the orange colors than the U.S. version. Scarce. $225.00 – 275.00.

"Fountains of Rome" (1962)

Color intensity is just a hair richer than the U.S. version. However, the central water movement at the top of the fountain on the primary side does not vary up and down like its counterpart. The European cylinder eliminates that effect but adds a slightly heavier water texture. $375.00 – 425.00.

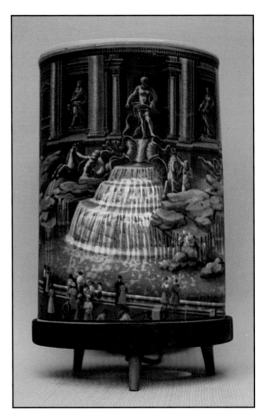

"Snow Scene – Church" (1957)

Practically identical to the U.S. oval version in scene quality, but curiously uses a totally different cylinder. The cylinder pattern is the same used on the "Sailing Ships" lamp from 1958 except the coloring used for waves at the bottom is omitted. This is the first example of an Econolite lamp having what later release Goodman lamps sometimes had — mismatched cylinders used most likely for expediency. Note the original box pictured, one of the very few known European boxes. Unfortunately, it has absolutely nothing printed on it. $200.00 – 250.00.

118

"A. Leuchten" Company

This is one of only two companies manufacturing motion lamps in Europe that labeled their lamps with a company name. This was definitely a German company, although the company used a logo and did not include a street address or list a city. The company numbered and named (in German) each of their motion lamps. All the lamps seen are round in shape with a characteristic hard brown plastic base and top. The lithography is quite good, and the finished product has a shiny L.A.Goodman-like quality to it.

There is a strong possibility that this company was somehow affiliated with the company producing gold topped Econolite lamps, as all three lamps ascribed to this manufacturer use the same blue cylinder described under the Fountains of Versailles. The only difference is that the fans were not produced from beer or oil can scraps. They are dissimilar, however, in that none of the lamps are marked with an Econolite or L.A. Goodman copyright or otherwise attribute their design motif to these two firms. These and all following European lamps are vintage 1950s – 1960s pieces.

"Alte Muehle" (Old Mill) #965

The graphic is definitely the Econolite scene, but there is no copyright marking. Scarce. $175.00 – 200.00.

"Wasserfall" (Niagara Falls) #962

A strange-looking lamp to the serious collector because it has the appearance of an Econolite but the style of a Goodman. Using a blue animation sleeve as well as a blue cylinder, when lit it shows as a very dark lamp with a decidedly greenish blue hue. Scarce. $150.00 – 175.00.

"Waterfall-Campfire"

There is no copyright or other attributing mark on the lamp although this is the only European lamp found using a Goodman scene. A very colorful lamp with the animation sleeve shining through in blue, mint green, and red. Very scarce. $175.00 – 200.00.

Unknown German Manufacturer

There is also a German firm that manufactured inferior copies of Econolite lamps as well as creating at least one new motif of its own. These lamps are characterized by a gold or bronze metal base that is copied from the Econolite design, although the metal used is flimsier than the Econolite version. In addition, the pivot rod arm on these lamps has a distinctive tuning fork shape to it which is actually an improvement over the Econolite design as this design always ensures that the cylinder is centered directly over the bulb and also better protects it from touching a hot bulb. This design includes the metal sleeve with a detachable point for better alignment as discussed above.

Generally speaking, these lamps were technically well constructed, particularly the cylinders. Where the quality breaks down is in the lithographic process. It appears that the company used some kind of color photo lithography which only reproduced the image on the outer surface of the shade and also produced a somewhat grainy and light colored result. As one can imagine, the effect is magnified when the lamps are lit and a clear bulb is used.

"Antique Car"

Identical graphic to the Econolite version. Curiously, instead of the names of the autos, the words "Made in Germany" are substituted. The lithographic color and quality are decidedly inferior to an original Econolite, yet the cylinder is well crafted. Scarce. $200.00 – 225.00.

"Apollo Brunnen – Versailles" (Fountains of Versailles)

The German word for fountain (Brunnen) is used and the words "C Fanta Plastic" are displayed prominently on the front side. The color quality is good but again, below the Econolite standard. Scarce. $375.00 – 425.00.

"Old Mill"

A photo-lithographic copy of the 1956 Econolite version. Bears the marking "Made in Germany." Scarce. $150.00 – 175.00.

"Schwarzwald Muhle" ("Black Forest Mill")

A quaint German motif with the front side featuring the front view of an old German mill house complete with waterwheel and flowing stream. The reverse features the back side of the house, from a distance, accentuating the Black Forest setting with a stream flowing in the foreground. An interesting lamp as the Black Forest region is found in the south of Germany while the style of house depicted, combined barn and farmhouse with thatched roof, is distinctively northern Germany. To further add to this interesting lamp, the quality of rendition gives the appearance that it was based upon an oil painting. The animation is rather soft. Desirable and extremely scarce. $250.00 – 300.00.

121

"Red Topped" Econolite Lamps

Yet another European firm manufactured lamps copied from the popular designs of the Econolite Corporation. These lamps are distinguished from their European counterparts by the hard plastic red top, a red plastic insert between the outer surface and animation sleeve at both the top and bottom, and a dark brown and gold filigree base. Aside from the plastic base which is functional but not as sturdy as the metal version, these are the best technically constructed lamps found thus far, including the original Econolite lamps. The pivot rod arm has the tuning fork shape along with the detachable metal sleeve. It appears that the photo-lithographic process was also used, but the quality and the colors are first rate. The only drawback, however, is that they are not printed on both sides of the outer shade surface. Still, the results are very good even when lit. Cylinders are the same as the American versions, although they use a slightly heavier plastic.

"Hearth"

The outer shade bears the markings "Econolite Corp. Litho 1958." An attractive and very scarce lamp. $225.00 – 275.00.

"Forest Fire"

Upon first inspection, this lamp appears to be identical to the 1955 Econolite version. A closer look, however, reveals that all the forest animals have been carefully removed from the scene. It is possible that animals in danger may have been offensive to the European market. Very scarce. $150.00 – 200.00.

122

"Lighthouses"

The design for this lamp is loosely based on the 1962 Econolite Lighthouse lamp. The German version appears to be copied from an oil painting of a similar scene. Both sides feature slightly different lighthouses on a rocky shore on a moonlit night. The motion effects in this lamp are some of the best found in the European lamps. Extremely scarce. $400.00 – 450.00.

"Old Mill"

Very similar to the 1956 Econolite Old Mill except the graphic is enhanced with lush colors and has the quality of an oil painting. The animation is less forceful, but the gorgeous color compensates. The base is marked "Fantaplastic." The red top in this example is made of cardboard. Very scarce. $200.00 – 250.00.

"Old Mill"

Identical to the Econolite 1961 Old Mill except this version has the dense, rich colors found on so many of the European lamps. The animation is a bit less forceful. Extremely scarce. $350.00 – 400.00.

Roto-Electric B.V.
Enschede, Holland

This is only the second European manufacturer to mark its lamps. The marking is stamped in raised letters on the bottom of the plastic base. The only lamp found thus far has been a psychedelic.

"Op Lamp"

This is the same design as the Visual Effects Inc. lamp. Scarce. $50.00 – 75.00.

Former East German Lamp Company

These lamps were probably made in East Germany during the time of the Cold War. The lamps manufactured by this firm are characterized by white plastic bases and tops. The cylinders, although varying in size, are all the same basic design. The construction is sturdy, yet the materials used are not of the greatest quality. In addition, the scenes used are from real photographs, and all depict some manner of water flow. Consequently, the motion effect achieved is rather plain and unimaginative. Given the historical time period and the likely country of origin represented by these lamps, they are quite fascinating.

"Stream in Meadow"

This lamp was made in both a 12" and a 14" tall version. The scene depicted is a stream in the foreground with a flower-filled meadow and forest for a backdrop. Very scarce. $200.00 – 250.00.

"Elbe River Stream"

This lamp was produced in at least two variations, one with a white plastic base and top and the other with a wooden base and top (probably the earlier version). Both variations are approximately 8" in height. The scene depicted is a stream from the Elbe River which is located in the former East Germany. Vary scarce. $200.00 – 250.00.

"Stream in Forest"

This lamp stands 14" tall. The scene depicted is a stream in the foreground running through a dense forest. Very scarce. $200.00 – 250.00.

"Nude Woman Bathing"

Water cascades over the body of a woman bather. The motion effect produced is the shower effect of the water. Somewhat risque, certainly unusual, and very scarce. $225.00 – 275.00.

Miscellaneous Lamps

These are European lamps that are not attributed to any of the other manufacturers.

"East German Miners Lamp"

This interesting lamp hails from the Erzgebirge (Ore Mountains) section of the former East Germany and stands about 8" tall. In the foreground are rather crudely drawn and colored trees and two deer. When lit, the entrance to a mine is visible at the top. Underneath, the cylinder spins with scenes depicting people in various types of work — a gamekeeper with a deer, a woman carrying pails of milk next to a cow, a man driving a horse-drawn carriage, a woman at a spinning wheel, and a miner standing beside two crossed hammers which is the symbol of miners. There is a written phrase, which loosely translated reads, "He gives everything for the Fatherland, very slowly the night creeps along, it is the end of the workday, the day's work has been accomplished." Very rare. $250.00 – 300.00.

"Danish Niagara Falls"

The design of this lamp is based on the 1955 Econolite rendition, but the lamp has a later Goodman look. The colors are primarily blue and white, creating a rather surreal effect. Scarce. $125.00 – 150.00.

"Fish Lamp"

This is a small tripod lamp that stands about 12" tall. It is modeled after the 1954 Econolite rendition although the quality of the artwork is inferior and the diameter is smaller. Very scarce. $175.00 – 200.00.

"Danish Forest Fire"

Fire rages in the forest. With its bold use of yellow and other colors, the graphic is a standout from a distance, but as one looks closer, the rather simplistic art quality is evident. Still, very interesting with one of the more unique looks for a forest fire. Prone to image flaking like some Goodman lamps. Very scarce. $175.00 – 200.00.

"Hearth"

An Econolite lamp that is marked "Made in Germany" on the animation sleeve. We include this since it seems to combine characteristics found in other lamps and then some. Not surprisingly, the litho is one-sided, the base has the tuning fork pivot rod support with adjustable point, and the cylinder has a vertical seam. But, the lamp and cylinder are numbered (773 Oval) and the Econolite name and date do not appear on the graphic but rather on the animation sleeve. The cardboard top is salmon-colored with a slight gold pattern. Other models like this must certainly exist. $175.00 – 225.00.

It would be great to ferret out more European lamps. By developing contacts in other countries, or by visiting and searching in person, we may uncover many more gems from countries all over the world. Who knows what rare and unusual lamps are out there just waiting to be discovered. A very recent example of such good fortune was the discovery on a business trip to Denmark by our collector friend Mike Myers of eight motion lamps in the very first antiques store he visited! We encouraged him to leave his home address and phone number with the Danish dealer for future finds. Descriptions of two of these outstanding lamps, Danish Antique Autos and The Little Mermaid, are in the More Motion Sickness chapter on page 246. Another lamp Mike found features the Tivoli Gardens with background fireworks. These Danish lamps have characteristics similar to the 1950s Goodman Lamps, much like the Danish Forest Fire shown on this page. What Fred Pribble and now Mike accomplished stand as examples we all might try to emulate. Bon voyage and good luck!!

❧ Other Lamp Manufacturers ❧

The companies covered in the preceding pages were the most recognized based on longevity, output, and quality. However, many other manufacturers have produced noteworthy, interesting motion lamps. Some have made a handful while others have made only one or two. We provide information for as many companies as we can, given the limited knowledge available for some rather obscure lamp makers. Some of these lamps have identifying names on the frameworks while others do not. We show here a great variety of themes grouped together. Several of these lamps are quite recent and a few are still in production.

Gritt

This Indianapolis, Indiana, based company is rather special since their lamps were always figural and were composed of plaster. Beautifully sculpted and hand painted, they are sturdy and appealing with their rainbow-like colors. However, animation-wise they simply offer flames; interesting, weaving pattern, realistic flames, but nonetheless just flames! Their lamps were given the name "Aladdin Fire-Fleck Action Lamps," and used a metal hood that clamped over the bulb and acted as both reflector and pivot point for the cylinder. Sometimes their cylinders were made of metal strips woven together, but often the cylinders were nothing more than simple metal fans. A metal reflector with etched black peaks formed the basis for a realistic flickering flame look when coupled with the light and motion of the spinning fan or cylinder. Very few other companies used this style of animation. The lamps produced are simple and sturdy and have survived well. Deteriorating paint on the surface of the flat glass scene panels is one of the minor problems facing today's collector of these. Missing lamp compartment covers may also be a problem since they merely sat on the rear with no mounting screws or hinges. We have documented seven lamps and one specialty lamp.

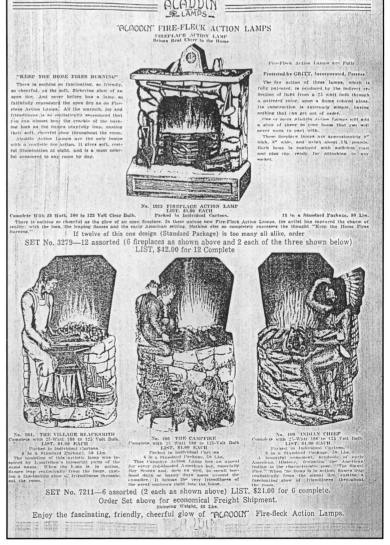

Indian Chief (1920s) #100
Flames fan out from the logs.

A bold and stately Indian chief is featured standing at a fire. Shows wonderful use of color. The chief can be mated with the Indian Maiden; they are designed to oppose each other. Fairly hard to find. $200.00 – 250.00.

Indian Maiden (1920s)
Flames fan out from the logs.

Somewhat harder to find than the Indian Chief described at left. $225.00 – 275.00.

Village Blacksmith (1920s) #104
Flames fan out from the hearth.

The figure standing by the fire is a muscular blacksmith. Harder to find than the Indians and even more colorful. A variation of this lamp features a three-dimensional blacksmith painted in fewer different and muted colors. A simple clip on the bulb holds a tiny fan that spins to create shadows of light that project through the holes in the hearth area and onto the glass. Possibly made by another company as a knock-off. $225.00 – 300.00.

Campfire (1920s) #106

Flames fan out from the logs.

Featured in this lamp is a Boy Scout. Quite rare in the Gritt series and a crossover collectible. Note that the shape of the glass pictured is incorrect. It should be the same shape as the Blacksmith lamp. $250.00 – 325.00.

"Campfire with Bugler" (1920s)

Flames fan out from the logs.

Featured in this lamp is not only a Boy Scout but also an opposing bugler. One of the rarest of the series and a crossover collectible. Note that the glass pictured is not the original shape but very pleasing and hard to cut this way. $275.00 – 350.00.

"Mt. Vesuvius" (1920s)

Flames billow out of the volcano while in the foreground the lake ripples.

One of the hardest to find in the series, and the only one to have an effect other than flames flickering. $275.00 – 325.00.

Fireplace (1920s) #1023

Flames flicker and the area under andirons glows.

Unusual for Gritt since this lamp uses a papier-mâché framework. Harder to find than most Gritt lamps, it features a unique internal construction that places the bulb sideways. Uses a metal fan and reflector similar to the Indians. The flames are bolder and wider than in most of their other lamps. It has a plastic window covering the hearth opening. $250.00 – 300.00.

"Chambersburg – 1861" (1930s?)

Fire blazes throughout a house.

This is the first in a series by Gritt called their "Flamotion Displays." Whether others were released is uncertain. The large unit features sturdy metal and glass construction. The lighted panel at the bottom is blank, so a company advertising fire insurance could place their name in the space. Rare. $400.00 – 500.00.

Metal Fireplace

Unidentified except for a patent number on the back covers, this series of lamps has inner parts that are very much like Gritt parts. But instead of plaster, all are cast metal and all are figural fireplaces with various characters placed before the fire. The animation is not realistic since the makers left out the animation glass, resulting in sideways moving "flames" as the cylinder spins. One very simply drawn animation glass would have vastly improved the action, or they might have used the Gritt system of reflector and spinning fan. It is hard to speculate why the manufacturer did not bother to improve the design since the construction is otherwise sturdy and shows quality. All include nice detail in the metalwork that renders them nearly as appealing when turned off. We have documented six lamps produced. All are 1930s releases.

"Man Reading Book and Large Dog Facing Him"

A lion sits on the mantel. Hard to find. $150.00 – 200.00.

"Man Reading Book and Small Dog Facing Fire"

A lion sits on the mantel. Hard to find. $150.00 – 200.00.

"Nude Children Before Fire"

A lion sits on the mantel. One child is standing, the other is seated. Probably the best of the series. Possibly patterned after early 1900s painting known as "After the Bath." Very scarce. $225.00 – 275.00

"Nude Child Before Fire"

A lion sits on the mantel. Same seated figure as above. Very scarce. $200.00 – 250.00.

"After the Bath"

"Man and Woman Seated at Fireplace"

A clock is on the mantel. The most common of the series. Man is smoking a pipe while the woman is knitting. Also released in scarce pewter finish with black highlights. $125.00 – 175.00.

"Man and Woman and Dog at Fireplace"

Probably not made by the same producer as all the others in the series, but very similar look except that it is only two dimensions rather than three. Rear construction less sturdy. Fairly hard to find. $125.00 – 175.00.

The rear covers of the metal fireplace lamps are often nicely detailed as shown. They slide up and off the base.

Ignition Company

The Ignition Company was located in Omaha, Nebraska, in the late 1940s. They produced only two known lamps, and these were rather cheaply made. They emitted a fairly dim animated image under normal light conditions. Their bulbs were coated with red or blue colors with small areas left open for light projection. Fortunately most of their special low wattage bulbs are still working because when they burn out, new ones have to be hand painted to achieve the proper animation. Had they used glass sleeves instead of cardboard, the animation might have been greatly improved. It is rather amusing that they offered a special blue bulb for 35¢ additional to those who had already purchased their Niagara Falls lamp (that was supplied with a red bulb as standard). Why not supply the blue bulb as standard equipment instead of supplying the red bulb used in their Forest Fire, when the blue bulb looks more natural in the Niagara Falls lamp? Curiously, the company offered an optional glass sleeve that would fit snugly over the outer shade and support the thin cardboard. Since this was 50¢ extra, or half the price of a complete lamp, few ordered it and the glass sleeves are rare today. Note that they did not use animation sleeves, but rather printed graphics in black on the inside of the scene sleeve to achieve similar yet cruder effects.

Forest Fire (1948)
Fire blazes in the forest.

Due to the comments listed above and also to a glass bead that is usually missing, this is a hard lamp to find working properly. We have discovered specially painted original bulbs of a higher wattage that enhance the animation considerably. Not too difficult to locate, as the original price was cheap even then! $100.00 – 150.00.

Niagara Falls (1948)
Water flows downward.

All above comments apply. These are much harder to find than the Forest Fire lamps, possibly because they are even duller to look at. Note that in all Ignition lamps the cast metal tops usually have small slits all around for heat emission, while some models only have four small rows of slits. $100.00 – 150.00.

Warner Brothers

This is a fun series of lamps featuring the Warner Brothers cartoon characters. They are dated 1970 – 1971 and produced in two distinct styles. One style offers a revolving scene interacting with an outer scene. The other style offers animation of the glimmering/glistening variety often found in liquor or advertising lamps. The former style was available with Sylvester and Tweety, or Elmer Fudd and Yosemite Sam, or the Roadrunner and Coyote. There could also be a Daffy Duck model. The latter style probably features the same characters, judging from an original box for the Roadrunner and Coyote that is numbered 1502 and has numbers 1501, 1503, and 1504 also listed. All were produced by Visual Effects Company, and most are hard to find in good condition since the scenes on the outer shade are very prone to flaking.

Roadrunner and Coyote (1970)

The ornery Coyote chases the poor Roadrunner as the cylinder passes by window openings.

Colorful and nicely drawn. Easiest lamp to find of a series that is not very easily found. $125.00 – 175.00.

Yosemite Sam and Elmer Fudd (1970)

Cylinder of Bugs Bunny running goes by window openings

Another colorful and nicely drawn lamp. Somewhat harder to find than above. $150.00 – 200.00.

Sylvester and Tweety
(1971)

Sylvester's eyes flicker and change color as does the lettering for the character names.

Circle patterns at bottom move. Hardest to find of the series. Richly drawn. $175.00 – 225.00.

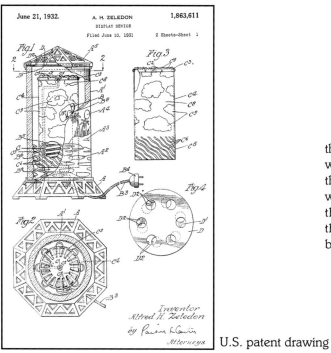

U.S. patent drawing

Roadrunner and Coyote
(1970)

The outlines of the characters sparkle and change color as do the words on patterns above and below.

Side one features the Roadrunner in flight while side two has two Roadrunners standing with Coyote nearby. Limited, but true animation. Very hard to find. $175.00 – 250.00.

Miscellaneous

This section covers lamps made by various companies that produced just one or only a few models, or companies whose lamps did not fit into another category. Some of these lamps have identifying names on the frameworks while others do not. You will see a great variety of themes which we have grouped together. Several of these lamps are quite recent and a few are currently being produced.

"Aladdinette Child's Lamp" (1925)

Small paper shade with characters spins around.

The earliest motion lamp included in this book, and one of only two known to be powered by oil and flame. It was made by Aladdin Industries and shaped like a candle holder. It is constructed of metal and paper. One style shows nursery rhyme characters and the other shows various animals on the shade. Quite scarce. $200.00 – 250.00.

"Candle Carousel – Marsh Ducks" (1980s)

Small paper shade with ducks spins around.

"Metal Lighthouse" (Late 1920s)

Multi-colored beacon top revolves.

Less than 6" tall, this lamp was originally powered by oil and flame, but it has been electrified for convenience. The base it sits on appears to be added. It may have served as an early model train set piece. $75.00 – 100.00.

Candlestick-shaped bases for spinning shades have been popular in recent years. Even though driven by electric generated heat, it is still much like the Aladdin lamp idea, proving that good motion lamps never really go out of fashion! $25.00 – 50.00.

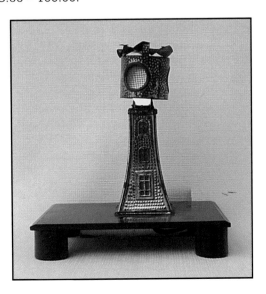 

"Green Glass Goldfish" (1930s)

Fish swim by.

Due to the shape of the green satin glass, the distortion form of animation takes place and images tend to look somewhat shadowy. The lamp features rugged construction with its fancy cast metal base and top. Tops are often missing, as are the glass bearings. They enjoy a fairly decent survival rate and are popular and desirable. $275.00 – 350.00.

"Ribbed Clear Glass Lamp" (1930s)

Flames spiral upward.

Identical metal framework to the Green Glass Goldfish lamp, except chrome plated. The orange and red cylinder inside gives a flame look that is rather simplistic which is a shame since otherwise it is an impressive-looking piece. Very scarce. $225.00 – 275.00.

"Deep Sea Fish" (1930s)
The water moves.

The cast metal, pewter finish framework features a bowed scene that includes two figural fish that stand out before the painted front glass. Closely behind this glass sits a glass panel that has sea foliage drawn on it that projects through when lit. Behind this sits a third glass panel that has a pattern molded into it which creates the animation lines. This lamp and the one that follows are the only known lamps that use three panels of glass with a molded scenic front. It is possible they were known as "Naggart" lamps, although we cannot be certain of this company name. Due to the construction, the animation has more noticeable depth. It is an interesting and seldom seen piece. $250.00 – 300.00.

"Jungle Forest Fire" (1930s)
Fire blazes.

Basic construction is identical to the lamp at left. The delicate pot metal front scene is missing a small fallen tree with an animal at its base. Note the cougar on the right and the snake wrapped around the tree on the left. The animation glass is thick and is marked with an L for left and R for right, as proper placement is important. The second glass panel for this lamp has trees drawn on it that project through when lit. The end result of the animation is a unique looking fire that is quite pleasing. As this book went to press, we were told there may be a third model using the same construction and having some sort of shadow effect for the animation. Very scarce. $250.00 – 300.00.

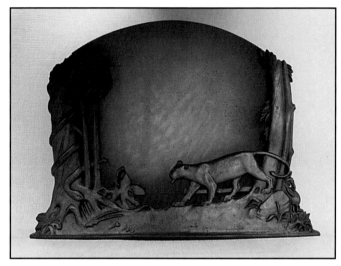

"Unique Lamp Company Marine Lamp" (1930s)

Action and scene are identical to Scene-in-Action Marine model. This is a tall and fancy lamp, very likely released in association with Scene-in-Action. It is possible other scenes were also used in this framework. Very scarce. $275.00 – 325.00.

"Forest Fire in Fancy Framework" (1930s)

Action and scene are identical to Scene-in-Action Forest Fire model. This lamp was probably released like the one opposite, but no company name appears on it. Finely detailed metalwork. Very scarce. $225.00 – 300.00.

"Aluminum Framework Marine Lamp" (1930s)

Action and scene are identical to Scene-in-Action Marine model. It features a distinctive style and was probably released in association with Scene-in-Action. Very scarce. $275.00 – 325.00.

"Proscenium Arch Boating Scene Lamps" (1931)
Water falls and flows downstream.

An imposing framework highlights this lamp which is otherwise a bit dull in animation. One graphic features a man and woman in flat bed boat with falls in the background while the other features a tugboat at the falls. The tugboat version has two waterfalls, while the flat bed boat version has only one waterfall. Note that the lamp framework was also released in a pierced version, which has openings at the columns and at the top. They feature the only conical-shaped cylinders we have seen. (See Proscenium Arch Indian lamp in More Motion Sickness chapter.) Scarce. $200.00 – 250.00.

141

"Round Boating Scene Lamp" (1931)

Water falls and flows downstream.

Uses identical graphic to first Proscenium Arch model on page 141. The cast metal is prone to warping. A very stately feature is the eagle crested top. The fancy pedestal base is also noteworthy. Again, conical cylinders are used. Also released with graphic identical to second Proscenium Arch model on previous page. Curiously, the round models are signed "Motion Electric Lamp Corporation 1931" but this information is usually cut off the Proscenium Arch lamps. Very scarce. $200.00 – 250.00.

"Elephant Lady Fortune Teller" (1930s)

Shadows flicker on the lady's face while jeweled prisms glow.

This is a particularly beautiful hand-painted figural piece that is made of plaster and mounted to a wood base. It was produced by S&S Mfg. Co. of Wisconsin. It is very Art Deco with teardrop prisms hanging from the elephants' snouts. The animation is provided by a tiny spinning metal fan inside the urn. Both this piece and a tiny metal incense cup that rested at the front of the base are often missing. Very scarce. Several model numbers have been documented with the same style and various colors as follows: #202-multi-colored; #203-black; and #207-red. $350.00 – 450.00.

"Fortune Teller" (1928)

Shadows flicker on the lady's face and arms.

This is another fine hand-painted figural piece that is made of plaster. There is a heavy cardboard base which must be unglued to change the light bulb, a very inconvenient design! The animation is provided by a tiny spinning metal fan and incense cup mechanism that is often missing. The metal fan holds colored plastic cells which don't seem to change color of the shadows today. Probably made by the Martin Novelty Company. Very scarce. $250.00 – 300.00.

"Lady with Hair Blowing in the Wind" (1928)

Shadows flicker on the lady's face.

This fine figural lamp is hand painted and made of plaster. Design-wise, the most interesting feature is how the figure's hair flows out to the right. All of the information about Fortune Teller applies. Quite scarce. $275.00 – 325.00.

Meditation (1928)

Shadows flicker on lady's face.

All of the information about Fortune Teller applies. Hardest to find of the series. $300.00 – 350.00.

"Deco Girl" (1930s?)
Colors swirl on glass behind girl.

A long cylinder causes the action. This is quite an unusual motion piece since there is a metal statue in front of the action. Extremely scarce. $175.00 – 225.00.

"Niagara Falls" (1930s)
Water falls and flows downstream.

From a distance, one would swear this is a Scene-in-Action standard round Niagara Falls lamp. But close inspection reveals an animation sleeve with a sky blue color rather than the usual dark blue and more important, a cardboard shade instead of the usual paper covered glass. The animation is inferior due to these differences. The metalwork is identical, so it may be a prototype or variation that saw little production. A forest fire model may also exist. Rare. $125.00 – 175.00.

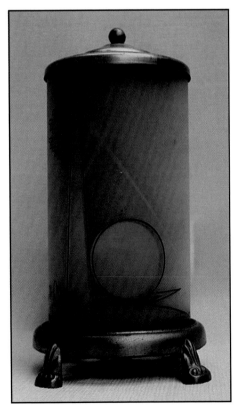

"1939 New York World's Fair" (1939)
Colors swirl around and beacons light.

The satin glass shade features a symbolic fair scene with the Trylon and Perisphere. It is only one-sided and has an inner animation sleeve made of paper. The action is rather meaningless, but this is an attractive and extremely rare lamp and crossover collectible. $350.00 – 400.00.

"Three Wise Men of Gotham/Winken, Blynken, and Nod" (1948)

Waves move around the boats.

This is an unusual lamp produced by the Lightcraft Company. It features a different theme for each side, but uses the same animation. The graphic is quite nice on this rare children's piece. $200.00 – 250.00.

"Little Jack Horner/Little Miss Muffet" (1948)

Flames flicker in the fireplaces.

All comments above apply. The framework of this example has been painted in a cream color. The original color is red. Rare. $200.00 – 250.00.

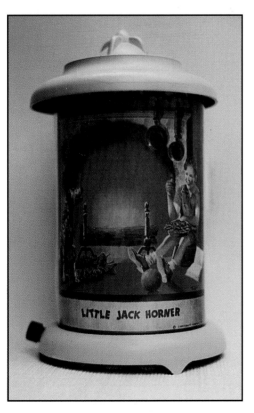

"Carousel Lamp" (1940s?)
Kids on a carousel spin by a window opening.

This is a very cute children's lamp that is quite delicate due to its paper shade and paper moving figures. The inner scene features a barker standing at an organ. Very scarce. $200.00 – 250.00.

"Forest Fire" (1940s)
Fire blazes in the forest.

The construction of this is similar to the Ignition Forest Fire except that the metalwork has no decoration and there is no animation marking on the inside of the paper scene. The color is less vivid and tends to blacks, which also gives the lamp poor animation. At first glance the graphic may look just like the Ignition model, but study will point out differences. Scarce. $100.00 – 125.00.

"Bakelite Framework Niagara Falls" (1940s?)
Water falls and churns.

A common image is enhanced with good looking brown Bakelite top and bottom. It uses plastic construction, and the animation is inferior to the Scene-in-Action Niagara Falls. One variation has a somewhat heavier framework and slightly different shape to the top, which is screwed down. Very scarce. $150.00 – 200.00.

"Bakelite Framework Forest Fire" (1940s?)

Fire blazes.

Very similar to the previous lamp, but with a forest fire scene. Very scarce. $150.00 – 200.00.

"Mountain Stream" (1940s?)

Water falls and stream flows.

A beautiful scene in a picture frame structure. There are no maker markings. Scarce. $175.00 – 225.00.

"Fountain of Youth" (1950s?)

A country boy is peeing into a lake that ripples on front, and on rear a waterfall flows and water below ripples.

Quite a nice graphic is used on this unmarked lamp. It uses a framework identical to the Roto-Vue, Jr. lamps. The swans on the rear side are possibly more interesting than the explorers found on most other rear sides of this theme while the white rabbit watching the boy is cuter than the typical green frog. Extremely scarce and hard to find in good condition due to scene flaking. $175.00 – 225.00.

"Forest Fire with Elk" (1950s)

Flames rise out of the trees while flame reflections appear on water that is flowing downstream.

An unidentified lamp with a framework identical to Roto-Vue, Jr. lamps. The elk is prominent on the graphic. This is probably a Canadian lamp since the cylinder has a straight vertical seam. Very scarce. $125.00 – 175.00.

Mardi Gras (1950s)

Images of pretty girls in various stages of undress spin by open windows.

This is a fun lamp with a pin-up appeal. The outer shade theme is quite colorful and jazzy but prone to flaking. The lamp was offered as a premium to people playing punch card games in stores. We discovered an example in an original box with lettering identical to the style used by Goodman for their Lacolite products; Goodman may have produced this lamp for the people marketing it. Very scarce. $300.00 – 350.00.

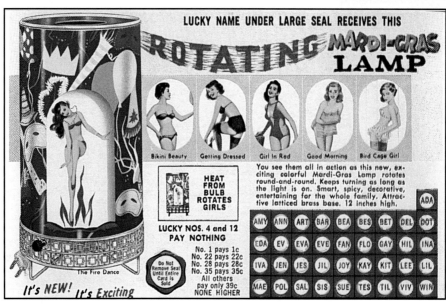

"Storybook Lamp" (1950s)

Pictures spin by window openings on either side.

Twelve color pictures make up a complete children's story with titles. Printed instructions on the heavy paper tell the user how to affix the story sheet to a large metal fan to form a cylinder. Different stories were probably available. The outer shade sits on a barbershop pole lamp base. Quite scarce. $250.00 – 300.00.

"Roy Rogers Rodeo Lamp" (1950s)

Scenes pass by a window opening.

Uses a framework like the Storybook Lamp and was made by Pearson Industries of Chicago. The large outer shade is heavy paper printed in color that features a rodeo scene that includes Roy Rogers twirling his lasso to rope a steer. The same scene is on the rear. The inner paper cylinder has nine different poses of Roy and his horse Trigger. The base and support pole are plastic and there are metal supports for the shade. Very scarce and desirable. $500.00 – 700.00.

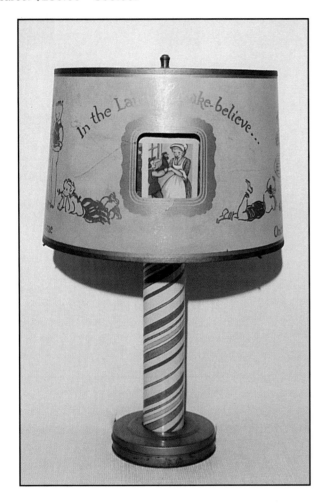

"Mary Had a Little Lamb" (1950s)

The shade spins around.

Similar to the Econolite Mother Goose but using a metal base, this lamp features an inner scene showing a teacher ringing a bell at a schoolhouse. Very scarce. $200.00 – 250.00.

"Ducks in Pond" (1950s)

Water ripples while clouds move above.

A very cute children's lamp that has a small rabbit sitting on its top and features some rabbits on the graphic. Produced by Marti of Hollywood and released in blue and pink. Very scarce. $175.00 – 225.00.

"Figural Lighthouse" (1950s)

Color beacon spins.

Made of plaster and unmarked, the lamp is not particularly attractive but is certainly unusual with a moving beacon. Scarce. $100.00 – 150.00.

"Forest Fire" (1950s)

Flames in forest blaze.

This is not as vivid as some other forest fires, but it features an interesting metal finger attached under the top that will keep the cylinder from popping off the pivot point. The top is held in place by screws. A variation of this lamp has the same scene and body color but a different construction in which the top is attached to the animation sleeve and scene. Very scarce. $125.00 – 175.00.

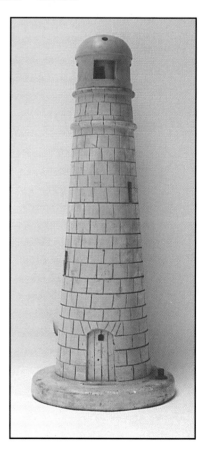

"Marx Revolving Beacon Tower" (1940s?)

The beacon spins around.

This was made to be used with Marx model trains. The beacon pivots on a special bulb with a flat glass top. It is powered by a train transformer. $25.00 – 40.00.

"Fireplace Logs" (1950s)

Flames flicker between the logs.

A colored cylinder gives off a somewhat phony fire look, but this unit is interesting since most of its type use a motorized rather than heat-driven cylinder. Fairly scarce. $50.00 – 75.00.

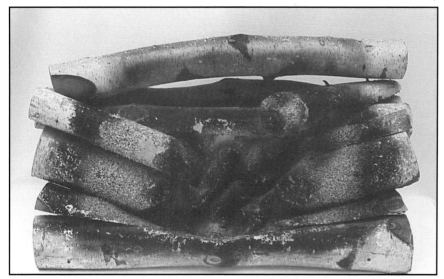

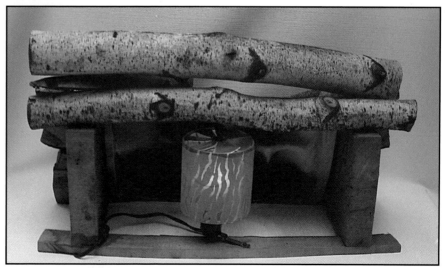

"Pedestal Niagara Falls" (1950s)

Water falls, churns, and flows downstream.

Probably foreign made with its vertical cut cylinder, the lamp has the pedestal style base and ball feet of Econolite, and the scene is identical to their Roto-Vue release. It is very possible that it was made under license from Econolite. The small scene size seems a bit out of place with the pedestal legs, giving a somewhat awkward look. It performs well though. Very scarce. $100.00 – 150.00.

"Niagara Falls" (1950S)

Water falls and flows downstream.

A lamp which looks very much like the Econolite Niagara Falls but features a metal top and bottom and a paper scene under a hard plastic outer sleeve. The animation sleeve is plastic, and the top screws on just like a jar lid. It has adjustable air holes in the top and a straight seam cylinder. Very scarce and possibly foreign. $100.00 – 150.00.

"Fish Lamp" (1950s)

Fish swim by.

A squat shade only 7" tall and 6" wide is formed with a pleated sleeve. It may be European and sits on three plastic feet. Very scarce. $125.00 – 175.00.

"Turkish Ladies Dancing" (1950s)

Women dance by.

Turkish wording on the outer shade and a pleated inner sleeve surround the cylinder. The outer sleeve is glass and sits on a metal base. Extremely scarce in U.S. $175.00 – 250.00.

"Ball and Sphere Lamps" (1960s – 1970s)

A cylinder casts color shadows onto the sphere which project onto walls or ceilings.

Individual prisms that make up the sphere act as reflectors while the cylinder provides the motion. The chrome finished plastic half-ball that forms the base also adds to the reflective quality of these lamps. A cousin of the psychedelic lamps, they were made in various sizes and somewhat different shapes. Radio Shack sold one very recently for about $19.95 and called it "Psycho Lite Color Show #42-3010." Scarcity depends on style. $35.00 – 60.00.

"Flying Saucer" (1970s)

Identical to the operation of the ball and sphere lamps on previous page, but shaped like a small flying saucer on three tiny legs. Fairly scarce. $35.00 – 50.00.

"Love Lamp" (1970s)

The shade spins around.

The word "love" in black letters appears on the shade in color. A very simple lamp that isn't often found. $50.00 – 75.00.

"Forever High" (1970s)

Words and images glisten and change color.

This lamp celebrates the ever popular marijuana plant. It is attractive and a true 1970s piece. Scarce. $100.00 – 150.00.

"King Royal" (1971)
Outlines of figures glimmer, water ripples, and flags wave.

Produced by Creative Lighting Division of Cheslak of California, the lamp features limited animation and cute cartoon like graphics on a small framework. Scarce. $100.00 – 125.00.

"Laurel and Hardy" (1971)
Cartoon-like images spin by window openings as bottom border flickers.

Produced by the same company as King Royal lamp to honor the famous comedians. The realistic outer shade is fine, but the cylinder graphics are rather simplistic and cartoon-like. Also, there are two slightly different cylinders we have seen used. Very scarce. The box will add to the value with this one. $200.00 – 300.00.

"Spirit of '76" (1973)

Outlines of figures and wording glisten and glimmer while some chimneys smoke.

Historic locations like Fort Ticonderoga and Valley Forge are shown in this medium-sized lamp by Creative Light Products. Limited animation in a very hard-to-find piece. $100.00 – 125.00.

"NHL Lamp" (1970s)

The National Hockey League logo glimmers while the hockey puck seems to travel from stick to goal.

The hockey player is surrounded by many team logos in this appealing sports lamp. Made by Visual Effects Co. Relatively scarce. $100.00 – 125.00.

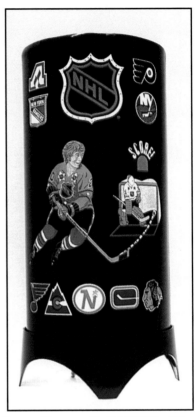

"Philadelphia Flyers" (1970s)

Flyers' logo glimmers while hockey puck travels from stick to goal.

The same images appear on both sides. Similar to NHL Lamp. Also made by Visual Effects Co. Relatively scarce. The sports lamps stand 13½" tall. $100.00 – 125.00.

"Ice Hockey Lamp" (1970s?)

Color blips move at top while hockey pucks and sticks glisten at bottom.

Similar construction and look as the Canadian lamps made by Monique. Scarce. $100.00 – 125.00.

"Outer Space" (1970s)

Color blips move in circles connecting objects like a space ship, man in space outfit, etc.

This is an interesting lamp because of its theme, but the animation could have been better. Very scarce. $150.00 – 175.00.

"Ballet Dancers" (1970s)

Color blips move in circles connecting the dancers.

Produced by the same company as Outer Space but unmarked. Men and women in colorful costumes look fine, but again the animation could have been better. Very scarce. $125.00 – 150.00.

"Leaves in the Wind" (1970s)

Color blips move in circles connecting leaves blowing in the wind.

Produced by the same company as above, and all three of their releases use the same cylinder. Very scarce. $125.00 – 150.00.

"Golden Coach Lamps" (1960s?)

Water moves or flames burn.

The appealing and fancy coach framework in plastic holds scenes on both sides and colored swirl panels at front and rear. Drawbacks include limited animation and themes that do not fit the look of the framework. One variation has fish swimming on one side and Indians at a campfire on the other. Another variation has Indians on both sides and still another variation has fish on one side and Niagara Falls on the other. Fairly scarce. $100.00 – 125.00.

"Fireplace" (1973)

Flames burn in a modern hearth.

The black background highlights the flames nicely. It has pretty good animation for a later lamp. It was produced by Creative Light Products. For five dollars additional, one could purchase a metal top for incense burning. Relatively scarce. $75.00 – 90.00.

"Cheers Nite Lite" (1970s)

Outlines of figures glimmer as do words that change color.

Produced by the same company as Fireplace on previous page, this is a very good bar lamp that features sexy girls in fishnet stockings. Not too hard to find. $100.00 – 125.00.

"Bar is Open with Glasses" (1970s)

Color blips move and drinking glass spin by.

This bar lamp is also eye catching but somewhat more tame than the one at left yet harder to find. $75.00 – 100.00.

"Bar is Open" (1970s)

Color blips move and words move as they change color.

This very popular bar lamp is eye catching. Made by Visual Effects Co. Fairly common. $50.00 – 75.00.

"Bar is Open with Barbershop Singers" (1979)

Musical notes and color blips flash at top and bottom while the beer mug foams and wording glistens and changes color. Outlines of singers glisten.

A lot is going on in this one! It sits on a raised metal base and was produced by Monique Display Enterprises, Inc. of Canada. The rear side says "bar is open" in French. Scarce. $100.00 – 125.00.

"Bar Lamp with Sexy Girls" (1979)

The word "bar" sparkles while outlines of girls and heads of beer glasses glisten. Tops of hanging spherical lamps above glow while drinks in glasses at bottom are connected by moving color blips. Bubbles all around change color.

Drink names from Mai Tai to Pina Colada and more are placed around lamp and some change color. There are also three sexy girls wearing heart-shaped outfits. There are a lot of little actions all going at once in this one. Produced by Monique Display Enterprises, Inc. of Canada. It sits on a raised metal base. Scarce. $100.00 – 125.00.

"Canadian Bar is Open" (1970s?)
Outlines of figures glisten.

Features large glasses holding drinks. Possibly made by Monique. Scarce. $100.00 – 125.00.

"Surfing Pacific" (1990s)
Color blips on top and bottom move while figures of sailboats and words glimmer.

An interesting graphic with an unusual inner cylinder that is black and white striped on the inner surface and color striped on the outer surface. Relatively hard to find. Made in China. $45.00 – 60.00.

"Bar is Open" (1990s)
Color blip patterns move at top and bottom while wording changes color.

Similar to the 1970s model but smaller in size, and with more interesting patterns above and below wording. Made in China by the same company that released the Surfing Pacific lamp. Very eye-catching. Relatively hard to find. $45.00 – 60.00.

"Pac-Man" (1980)
Name at top glistens, figures in grid glisten, and figures at top and bottom seem to travel from left to right.

A fun lamp produced by Bally Midway Mfg. Co. in honor of one of the most popular video games of all time. Both sides are identical. Original box includes picture of lamp. Scarce. $125.00 – 150.00.

"Annie" (1981)

The shade spins around. Colorful figures from the motion picture Annie spin by.

The white background stands in nice contrast to the images. Released by William F. B. Johnson Co. of Philadelphia, Pa. Not hard to find and often in an original box that has the lamp pictured. $50.00 – 75.00.

"Strawberry Shortcake" (1982)

The shade spins around.

Strawberry Shortcake characters fill the lamp in color tones that are familiar. It is copyrighted by American Greetings Corp. and the words "fun is all around" appear at the bottom. Released by William F. B. Johnson Co. of Philadelphia, Pa., and fairly scarce. Also comes in an original box that has the lamp pictured. $75.00 – 100.00.

"Japanese Tassel Lamps" (1960s?)

Figures spin around.

Most of the lamps in this series use a very similar plastic framework on legs with translucent windows and open-mouthed dragons holding tassels. The cylinders spin by very fast and often feature dragons. Some that are more unusual will feature people dancing. They use odd-sized bulbs that are somewhat hard-to-find. Fairly common. $25.00 – 40.00.

162

"Japanese Three-Way Merry Lamps" (1950s?)

Fish swim by.

These are odd-looking table lamps which use corrugated blue glass shades to produce motion by distortion. Some have metal tops with punched out letters that say "Merry Lamp." A pull of the chain illuminates the motion portion while another pull illuminates the lower glass portion holding imitation flowers nestled near a flower-shaped bulb. Take care of this bulb as they are nearly impossible to find. A third pull of the chain will illuminate both portions. A similar unit features the same animation structure but only a non-illuminated glass portion at the bottom that contains imitation flowers. Another variation features a similar animation unit sitting next to a tubular bulb with figural flower filaments that glow in colors. Sailboat cylinders exist and there may be other themes for these lamps. Scarce. $175.00 – 225.00.

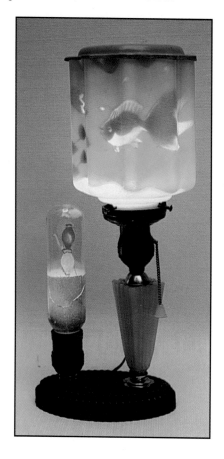

"Japanese Miniature Table Lamps" (1960s – 1990s)

A tiny cylinder projects images that spin around.

Many variations of theme and minor style changes were produced. All use a tiny pleated shade for the distortion effect. Fish were a popular theme. Some were even used to advertise places like Hawaii or Florida. The older ones are fairly scarce. $25.00 – 50.00.

"Japanese Pagoda Style Lamps" (1950s)

A scenic cylinder spins around.

Made of wood and silk-covered metal framework, these are interesting looking lamps. Cylinder themes vary from the common dragons to harbor scenes. Not easily found. $125.00 – 200.00.

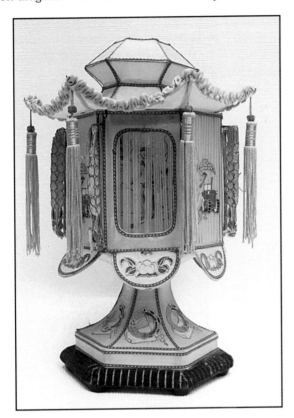

"Japanese Pagoda Music Box Lamps" (1960s)
Fish or scenic cylinder spins around.

Made of wood, metal, and plastic, these are cute but rather odd lamps. They are usually hand decorated over black lacquer and include a geisha figure that you wind to hear the music. The lamp inside lights the pagoda, the lamp to one side lights, and the motion unit lamp at top lights depending on the pull of the chain. Some models have a flip-type calendar instead of the side light. They often are missing the cylinder and shade since these are fragile and not attached. $150.00 – 175.00 if complete.

"Japanese Musical Aquarium" (1960s?)
Fish swim by rock formations.

This unit stands 15" tall and is 8" in diameter. The large blue encased glass shade has ten ribs and is heavy. Two cylinders are inside. One is a large cylinder with fish and the smaller inner cylinder has paper glued on to imitate rock formations. The cylinders spin in opposite directions for the effects. To really add an odd touch, you wind the music box in the metal base and it plays the "Anniversary Waltz". Our example is missing the fancy metal top. You could mistake this lamp for a small water cooler from a distance!! Very scarce. $225.00 – 275.00.

165

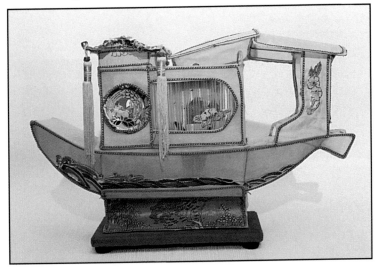

"Figural Silk Oriental Boat" (1960s?)

Sailboats pass by.

This pretty figural piece has a tiny cylinder that hides under the enclosed area of the vessel. Scarce. $75.00 – 125.00.

"Figural Plastic Oriental Boat" (1960s?)

Oriental figures, including rickshaw, spin around.

The boat has a lighted lantern at one end, and the passenger compartment flips up to reveal the cylinder. Scarce. $75.00 – 100.00.

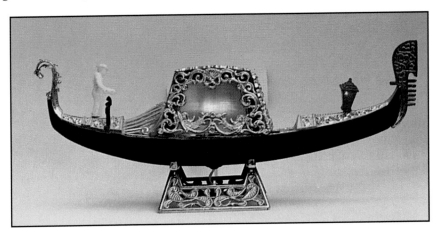

"Oriental Figure Holding Motion Unit" (1950s?)

Sailboats near harbor at Hong Kong move by.

Rather unusual lamp in that a statue supports the shade and motion unit. Scarce. $125.00 – 175.00.

"Japanese Hanging Lamps" (1960s to present)

Typical theme cylinders spin around.

Sizes of these lamps vary from small (about 10" tall) to medium (about 15") to large (over 20"). Usually very ornate, tassel sizes and styles also vary. Some recent examples that are about 30" tall even add blinking mini lights to the already dazzling colors and motion. Most feature plastic construction with silk often used for the animation screen. The example at bottom left is unusual since it is made entirely of silk over a metal frame and includes a huge hand-painted paper cylinder that is powered by dual light bulbs. Relatively scarce. $50.00 – 125.00 depending on size. Large silk model, $175.00 – 225.00.

"Santa Claus with Santa Shade" (1920s)

The colorful shade spins around.

This piece was produced by Unger and called a "Cell-u-pon." The papier-mâché Santa supports a bulb and the spinning paper shade with graphics and trim. This is a rare and exceptionally lovely Christmas collectible and motion lamp. $400.00 – 450.00.

"Christmas Night Lite" (1972)

Santa and his reindeer fly by overhead while words and figures on the lamp sparkle and change color. The rear side has a fireplace that burns and a Christmas tree that sparkles.

Produced by Creative Light Products of California, this lamp has the words "Merry Christmas" featured in different languages across the top. The front side is an exterior scene of houses in winter that are lined with Christmas lights and a lamppost that glows. The rear side is an interior scene that shows Santa and his reindeer flying by (observed through windows of the house). Kids are shown by a glowing Christmas tree and a burning fireplace. There is a lot going on in this lamp! It apparently was not widely distributed, making it somewhat hard to find. Several dozen survived a fire in a Pennsylvania warehouse, so many of these are mint in the box. $125.00 – 175.00.

168

"Star Christmas Tree Top" (1960s?)

A colorful cylinder reflects onto a prism-like ball and projects outward.

This unit was designed to sit on a tree or rest on a stand on a shelf. Not too hard to find. $20.00 – 40.00.

Heavenly Reflecting Light (1950s)

A shell behind the angel lights and flickers.

Designed to be placed on top of a tree, the light has a pivot that supports a simple plastic fan which spins to produce the flickering. Produced by the Bradford Company and sold originally for $1.98. Not too hard to find. $20.00 – 35.00.

Turbo Evergleam Four Color Projector (1960s) #4993

A drum with colored cells rotates.

Produced by the Aluminum Specialty Company of Wisconsin, this unit was designed to cast color shadows onto the then-popular aluminum artificial Christmas trees. Most units of this type were motorized, making this more unusual. Designed for use on the floor, wall, or table and supplied with a 150-watt reflector bulb. Fairly scarce. $25.00 – 50.00.

Evergleam Revolving Four Color Projector (1960s) #4992

Cylinder with colored cells rotates.

Produced by the Aluminum Specialty Company of Wisconsin, this much smaller unit than the previous one uses a 100-watt bulb behind a reflector and was designed primarily for table use. $20.00 – 35.00.

"Merry Christmas" (1970s?)

The shade spins around.

Cartoon-like Santa and reindeer graphic spins. It was cheaply made as the reverse side has words "Merry Christmas" backwards! Fairly scarce. $50.00 – 75.00.

Electric Christmas Rotating TV Lamp (1970s?)

Santa and reindeer spin by.

A squat winter scene outer shade frames the Santa spinning cylinder. Made in Hong Kong and available in red or green. Fairly scarce. $75.00 – 100.00.

Twink – L – Lite #14 (1940s?)

Pinpoints of light project and sparkle as tree spins around.

This is one of very few Christmas trees that uses an animation cone sleeve inside. Produced by Mirostar Products, Inc. of Patterson, New Jersey, it has a bottom cardboard-supported base that looks like a paper plate and is marked "Diamond Match Company." The sparkle effect is captivating, especially in a darkened room. Very scarce. Approximately 15" from base to tip. $150.00 – 225.00.

REVOLVING TWINK-L-LITE CHRISTMAS TREE INSTRUCTIONS

Remove unit from carton.

Remove both shades and discard cardboard disc (4).

Fit white reflector (3) on socket and frame. (2)

Remove needle set (5) from this instruction sheet and place on top of wire form.

Place in socket a 40 watt bulb for the No. 14 models and a 75 watt bulb for the No. 22 models.

Place black slotted shade (6) on frame first.

Near the tip of the outer shade (7) open up the die cut vents. (8)

Look up in the inside of the outer shade (7) and you will see imbedded in the plastic a brass fitting which holds a jewel. When placing the shade on to the needle, *make sure that the point of the needle fits into the jewel.*

Lamp will revolve best on a level surface and is most effective in a dimly lit area.

The Original

TWINK-L-ITE

Revolving Christmas Tree

Patent Pending

MIROSTAR PRODUCTS, INC.
50 Spruce Street
Patterson, N. J.

"Christmas Tree with Dots of Light and Colored Stars" (1940s?)

Pinpoints of light sparkle and project as colored stars glisten.

Similar in construction to the above, but with small various colored celluloid strips pasted under pierced star patterns for added neat light effects. Approximately 22" in height and made of thin cardboard. Very scarce. $175.00 – 225.00.

"Skaters Christmas Tree" (1940s)

The tree spins around.

Produced by Glolite, the handsome tree features graphics of ice skaters. There are boys, girls, and couples featured at the bottom of the green-colored tree. A yellow plastic star graces the top. Released only in the 15" size, and supplied with a red plastic base. Relatively hard to find. $125.00 – 175.00.

"Christmas Tree with Tiny Balls" (1940s)

The tree spins around.

Similar in construction to the Econolite trees except for tiny balls lining the bottom of the tree. Also, the trees are decorated with garlands and ornaments. Released only in the 15" size with a raised plastic base. We have found it in three colors: white, maroon red, and green. Relatively hard to find. $150.00 – 175.00.

"Christmas Tree of Heavy Cardboard" (1940s)

Tree spins around.

Uses more rugged construction than most and a somewhat different internal pivot support design. Unusual flocked surface on this medium-sized tree. $125.00 – 150.00.

Illumy Revolving Lights (1985)

Various cylinders spin around.

This series of lamps was produced by Midori Ltd. of Japan and imported by Midori Gifts of California. Spencer Gift stores carried them. They are among the very few square motion lamps. The milky-white shades use the distortion effect for animation. Note that there are two pivot rods that form a U-shape at the top to support the pivot point. This prevents the cylinders from touching hot bulbs, much like some of the European lamps. Another protective feature they share is twist and lock shades. The lamps were available with the following themes: Seaside #65033-001; Night View #65034-001; Dolphin #65035-001; Merry Go Round #65036-001; and Planet #65037-001. Some are better than others in their performance. They originally sold for $44.95. All are now relatively scarce. $100.00 – 140.00.

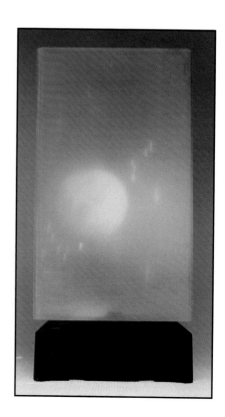

Illumy Lamps (1985)

Various cylinders spin around.

Also produced by Midori Ltd., these adorable little plastic lamps are part figural and therefore out of the ordinary. All have a triangular-shaped shade housing the cylinder. Figures that continue the cylinder theme stand next to the shade. Four models were produced, the Carousel, New York City, Hawaii, and Bridge and City. (See More Motion Sickness chapter for a fifth style.) Fairly hard to find now. $90.00 – 125.00.

Pearl Revolving Lamp (1990s)

Fish swim by and cast reflections.

The pleasing design of a goldtone open seashell with a silver color interior combines with an inner "pearl" assembly that houses the cylinder. This is a nice night light as well as an effective motion lamp. Made in Taiwan and originally sold for about $29.95. Currently easy to find. $35.00 – 50.00.

Shadowy Stand (1990s)

The same fish motion unit as pictured at left, only on a stand with two legs. $35.00 – 45.00.

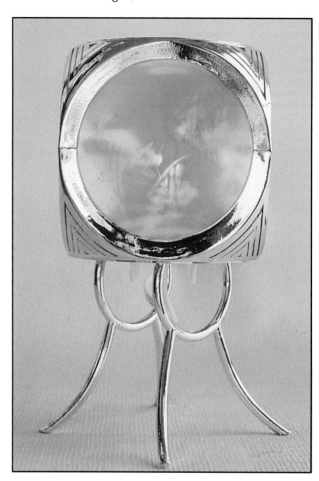

Antique Cart Lamp (1990s)

Fish swim by and cast reflections or dragons swim by and cast reflections, depending on which cylinder was originally supplied.

The same motion unit as used in Shadowy Stand is supported by a rickshaw-shaped base. Harder to find than lamps above. $35.00 – 45.00.

Harmony Lantern Lamps (1990s)

Cylinders cast images onto a square paper surface.

Made of wood and a rice paper covering, these lamps have been popular in specialty stores and are still being sold. Over 50 different cylinders have been available with images ranging from hot air balloons to teddy bears and can be purchased separately for about $24.95. The complete lamps sell for approximately $79.95. We have seen several used in recent motion pictures like the 1996 Sally Field film *Eye For An Eye* the 1996 Robert Redford-Michelle Pfeiffer film *Up Close and Personal*, and the 1996 Elisabeth Shue-Kyle Maclachlan film *Trigger Effect*. In fact, in its short life, this may have become one of the lamp styles most often seen on the silver screen. $80.00 – 100.00.

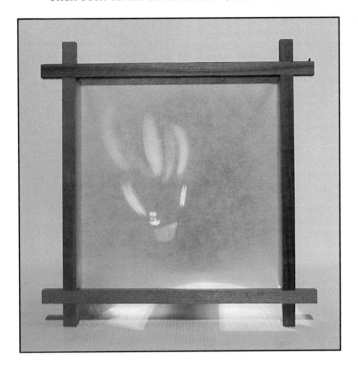 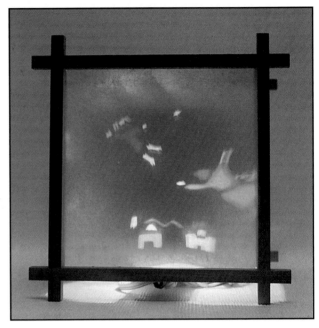

Tricycle Lamps (1996)

Spinning cylinders cast images onto outer sleeve.

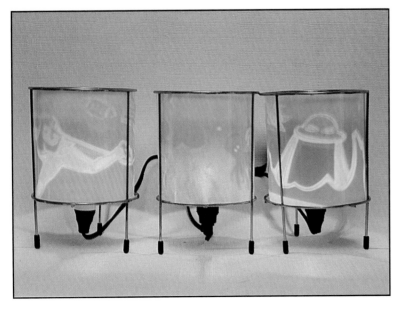

Made in Britain and featuring work by artist Shiu-Kay Kan, there are approximately 16 different themes available to date, Bubbles, Disco, Sea Life, Space Invaders, Love, Football, Soccer, Baby Spacemen, Hot Air Balloons, Scuba Diver, Ghost, Jazz, Night Scene, Sheep Over Fence, Squares, Teddy Bears, and Underwater. Some specialty models have been produced for commercial purposes including movie and cigarette companies. They are sold in mail order catalogues and stores for $44.95. Even though cute in shape, they are somewhat disappointing because the shade is not pleated, giving no real motion effect other than spinning. We hope they improve their designs in the future and also try to market them with light bulbs included. Produced and distributed by SKK Lighting of New Jersey. $50.00 mint in box.

Carousel Lamps (1996) #100, #200, #300, #400 series

Spinning cylinders cast images onto white bisque porcelain surfaces.

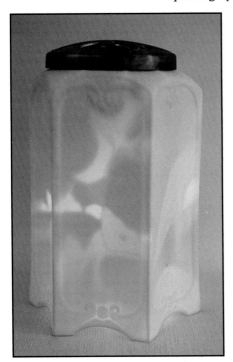

Possibly the nicest of the current lamps, the #300 series features a porcelain housing that is well designed and looks like a much older lamp. Inner cylinders are colorful, contain their own pivot points, and pivot on surfaces that should last a long time. Made in Toronto by Starry Nights Company. Sixteen different themes are available, Hummingbirds, Merry Go Round, Angels, Sun/Moon, Dinosaurs, Outer Space, Cow/Moon, Dolphins, Wild Horses, Winter Sleigh, Wedding, Butterflies, Halloween, Tropical Fish, Calico Cats, and one of our favorites, Santa Claus. Sold in mail order catalogues and gift shops for $60.00. There are also three other housings available that are simpler, less costly, and not as beautiful as the ceramic unit. The #100 series Oval Pine features a white oval parchment-like shade that is accented with a pine wood top and bottom. It is somewhat reminiscent of an oval Econolite lamp. It sells for $50.00. The #400 series is their Classic Oval that features the same oval shape and material as the #100 series, but is shaped over a metal frame and has no top or bottom covering. It sells for $40.00. Finally, the #200 series pleated model is a smaller lamp constructed for economy and features plain pleated parchment over a modest wire rim base. It sells for $37.00. Note that the buyer can choose any available cylinder theme for any one of the lamp housings for variety. Each cylinder, or insert as the company calls it, is available for $10.00. (Important note: We have found that most novelty lamps appear on the primary market for only a year or two, so it is wise to buy any new releases when you see them rather than wait.) If production ceases, these should be good future collectibles with value from $60.00 – 90.00 and more.

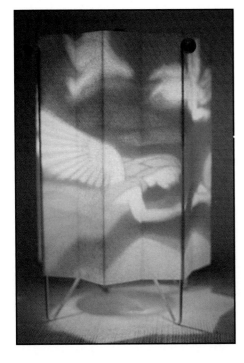

Light Show Lamp Kit (1996)

Vehicles pass by or fish swim around.

Produced by Patail Enterprises, Inc., the square plastic lamp has to be assembled by the buyer, and assembly was not that easy. Two different cylinders are included, one is fish, the other is different vehicles. Advertised as an "Arts and Science Project with two art cylinders – Ocean and Transportation." Works similar to the Harmony Lantern Lamps. Sold for $19.95

"Noah's Ark" (1997)

The shade spins around.

The Spin Shade Company has just released this fine new figural children's lamp. The base is beautifully formed and colored and is topped with a sturdy cardboard shade with appealing graphics. A nice refinement is the use of the pivot point within the shade, eliminating the chance of a sharp point piercing a paper shade. A small cup attached to a spring wire that hugs the bulb accepts the pivot point nicely. The retail price is $29.95. Expect that to go up in value when they are no longer available.

"Sleepy Time" (1997)

The shade spins around.

Same as the Noah lamp above but with the theme of animals in bed. The shade is pierced with star and moon patterns that sparkle as the shade revolves. The retail price is $29.95. Two different colored shades are available.

"Fireplace Grate Motion Units" (1930s?)
Coals glow and glisten.

These units were designed to be set into a fireplace to give the illusion of real embers burning. The largest one we have discovered is made by Peerless (possibly the same company that made the fine stoves). It has three spinning fans that sit above pivot rods near the bulbs. A wire mesh holds the pieces of glass cut and darkened to resemble embers. A smaller unit has only one fan in the center underneath the wire mesh. An example we spotted in a flea market had five fans encased in a separate cage under the wire mesh. We just missed one model that also had a built-in heater as well as metal fans that spin. An unusual unit called the "Magical Plus" was made by Berry's Electric Limited of England. It has two fans that are counter-rotating with pivot rods next to the bulbs. The embers are made of papier-mâché over a cheesecloth structure. Generally hard to find. $125.00 – 250.00.

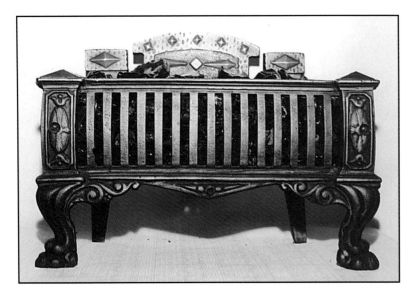

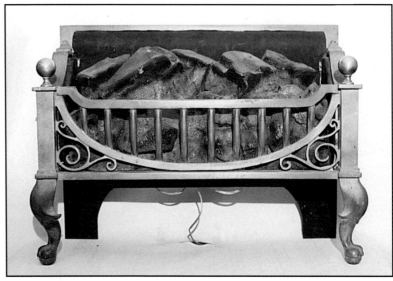

Radiovision (1940s)

Clouds shift as water ripples around the New York harbor.

A large and prominent battleship, fighter planes, and the Statue of Liberty highlight the scene that is set into the upper half of a wood "tombstone" style radio made around World War II. This is a great piece, since you can watch the action while the radio plays your favorite AM station. This crossover collectible took the original radio lamp idea to its ultimate conclusion by building the lamp right into the receiving set. Quite scarce. $500.00 – 750.00.

"Mermaid Clock" (1950s)

Fish and a mermaid pass by.

Produced by Dodge, Inc., this interesting piece is included since it is one of the only animated clocks we have seen that features a cylinder driven by the heat of the enclosed bulb. The Sessions Co. clock above the animation unit is motor driven. Beautiful figural unit using the distortion form of animation. The plastic front piece is usually fragile and brittle with age. A switch lights the optional animation. Very hard to find. $325.00 – 400.00.

Spinning Shades, Glo-Spinner Lamps, and Motion Ornaments

As early as the 1930s and continuing to the present, small spinning shades have been popular motion pieces. Mostly used on trees or electric candles at Christmas, they were made in quite a variety of colors and images. All are designed to pivot on a metal rod or paper cone with a metal point that could attach to a standard size Christmas bulb. Most shades are paper while some are plastic. A few plastic units were designed to sit above a bulb and the heat would spin a blade or figure in the center. These are actually motion ornaments.

Products called "Spin Shades" are currently in production with a pleasing variety of themes and some are shown in a store display we obtained. Their pivot points often need to be sharpened to work properly so be prepared to do a little filing. See larger display of these on page 184.

The Glo-Spinner Lamps pivot on a plastic base with a metal rod that is very similar to the earlier Econolite Christmas tree bases. The paper quality is not as good as the earlier lamps, and this results in a better look off than when on. However, their most interesting design is the witch since she even has a separate piece of paper that forms her hat and gives a more dimensional look! Try using different colored bulbs in these lamps to enhance their beauty.

Spinning Shades

Whirl-Glo Shades (1930s)

These were the best selling spinning shades of their time judging by the number that turn up today. Produced by the Sail-Me Company of Chicago. Using mostly Christmas themes, they were packaged in red and green boxes and were available in one large box of 10 or two small boxes with four different shades in each box. They are made of paper that has held up well and are topped with a brass pivot cup. Included are heat-resistant paper cones that hold thin, pin-like pivot rods. Special instructions on some boxes suggest that the user scrape the paint off the flame-shaped bulbs, on which the paper cones sat, for vivid light effects. Suggestions as to which color bulb would suit which shade and suggestions to prick tiny holes in certain shades for light sparkle were also included. More often than not, the pivot pieces are missing or damaged, but they can be hand made fairly easily. $3.50 each, $20.00 for box of four, $50.00 for box of 10.

Shadettes (1930s)

Much harder to find are these plastic shades with colorful lithos. Produced by Art Plastic Co. of Woodside, N.Y. They are very well constructed with metal fan tops and corresponding pivot cups. All these are Christmas, including Santa and trees, manger scene, etc. Sturdy metal pivot rods are included in the box of six. $4.50 each, $40.00 for box of six.

Gyro-Shades (1930s)

Shaped like small paper drinking cups, these are also hard to find. Produced by Sunbeam Specialty Co. of Cleveland, Ohio, they feature Christmas themes. Sturdily constructed with heavy paper, metal fan tops, and surprisingly, glass bearings. Each box contained eight shades and corresponding metal pivot rods. $5.00 each, $50.00 for box of eight.

Merry Go-Lites (1940s?)

These are the most unusual spinning shades with their color swirl patterns. Made by Deubener Shopping Bag Company of Indianapolis, they are nicely constructed of cardboard. They feature tiny holes for dots of light to sparkle through and have colored cellulose strips glued at intervals inside. Fans are cardboard and again, surprisingly, have glass bearings. Metal pivot rods are included. We do not have the box for these. $4.00 each, add a few dollars for box.

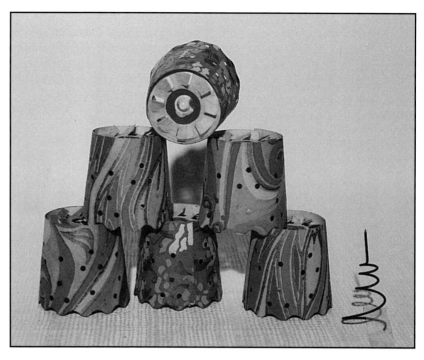

Glo-Spinner Shades and Lamps

Glo-Spinner products started appearing around 1994 and were made by the Daisy Kingdom Company of Portland, Oregon. They actually borrowed an original 15" Econolite Christmas tree to copy for their designs. They released six 16³/₈" tall tree-shaped lamps that included Frontier Santa, Tartan Floral, Bear Tree, Armful of Joy, Here Comes Santa Claus, Heavenly Angels, and the unique Halloween Selene Witch. Somewhat later in their production, they introduced mini tree-shaped shades that measured 5¹/₄" in height. These had the same graphics as the tree lamps and were packaged with pivot rods. The tree lamps sold for $19.95 and the mini trees sold for $7.95. We understand that the company is no longer producing any of these products, so they are already appearing on the secondary market at higher prices. $35.00 – 50.00 for large trees, $10.00 – 15.00 for small trees.

Spin Shades (1990s)

Spin Shades are made in China by the Spin Shade Company of Ventura, Calif. They started production several years ago and have grown steadily to where they now offer over 60 different spinning shades in a variety of themes from Christmas to Thanksgiving and special occasions like birthdays. They are patterned after the old Whirl-Glo shades from their shape right down to their brass pivot cups. They are sold individually, packed in boxes of three of a kind, in boxes of three with bulbs and cord, and in boxes with electric candles. Individual shades list for $4.95 and go up accordingly. Usually they are heavily discounted after the holidays are past, so look for bargains.

Motion Ornaments

Star Shaped

These ornaments are colored red, green, and white. They are plastic and include built-in fans that spin when hung over Christmas tree light bulbs. Fairly hard to find. $5.00 each, add several dollars if boxed.

Conical Shaped

These ornaments are colored red and white (possibly green and blue ones also exist). Designed to be hung over Christmas tree light bulbs, they include tiny plastic angels that spin above metal fans inside. Fairly hard to find $7.00 each, add several dollars if boxed.

Gazebo Shaped

These ornaments are colored green and pink and were made by Twinkle Toy Company of Youngstown, Ohio. A built-in fan spins in these as the above. Named "Christmas Tree Twinklers," they were sold in packages of four. Fairly hard to find. $6.00 each, add several dollars if boxed.

Psychedelic Lamps

These lamps, produced mostly in the early 1970s by Visual Effects Co., Inc., are in a class by themselves. The company called them "Op Lamps," short for optical lamps. The animation does not concern realistic scenes but rather patterns of color that move and change shape while teasing the eyes and senses. They were popular along with black light posters and other mind-bending items popularized by the hippies and flower children of the 1960s and 1970s. They can be mesmerizing to watch, and they frequently seem to attract collectors who do not desire regular motion lamps. They generally stand about 13½", with some a few inches shorter. The simpler ones use black and white patterns and the more complex ones employ color. Later lamps were released with two cylinders rotating in opposite directions for the psychedelic effects. The process used to apply the colors was probably not as permanent as the process used for standard lamps since image flaking seems more common in these. Surround yourself with a group of the psychedelic lamps working at the same time and you might get dizzy! We document 30 different models. Unless noted, all models shown are valued at $75.00 – 125.00 each.

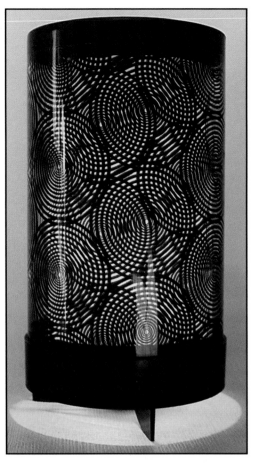
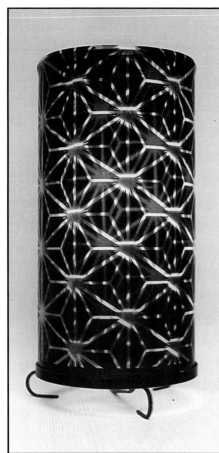

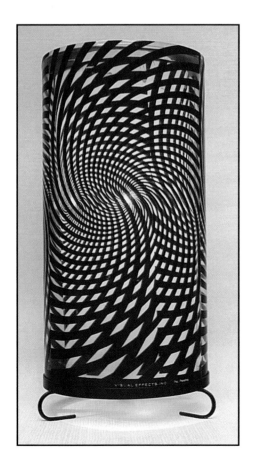
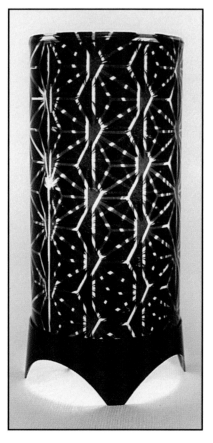

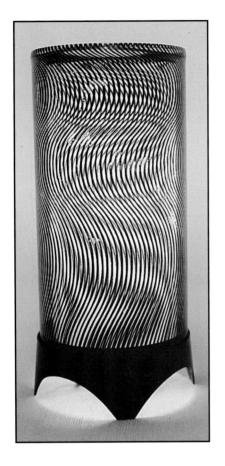

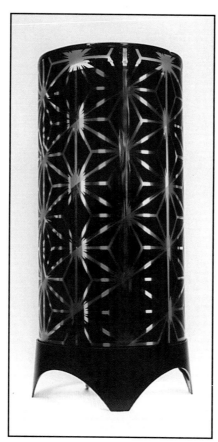

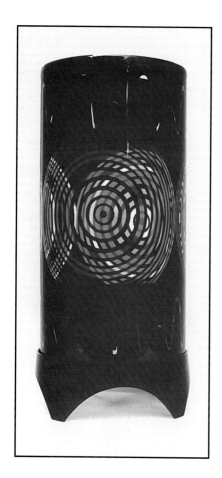

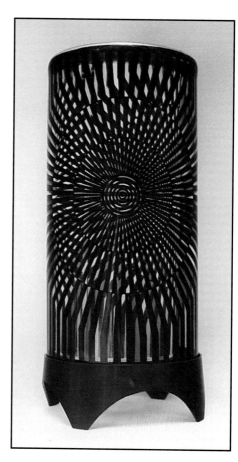

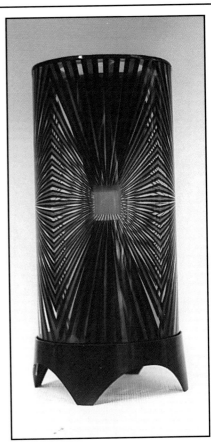

"Square Psychedelic Lamp" (1970s)
Color patterns move about.

This is an unusual framework and design since it features a chrome-colored circle layout that lines all four sides. The effect is more subtle than the standard psychedelics. Hard to find. $75.00 – 100.00.

"Six-Sided Psychedelic Lamp" (1970s)

Similar to the lamp at left, but with six sides instead of four. It was made in Denmark and also is hard to keep clean with all its crevices! Hard to find. $75.00 – 100.00.

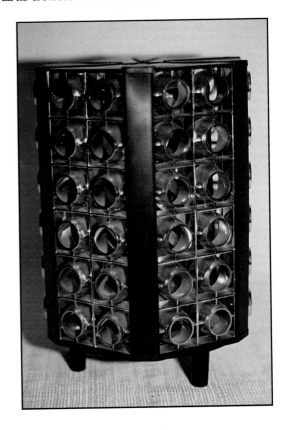

"Dual Cylinder Psychedelic Lamps" (1970s)

Colorful patterns swirl and dazzle the eye.

This is a unique design with an inner cylinder spinning one direction and an outer cylinder spinning in the opposite direction. The resulting images are projected onto a white outer sleeve which unfortunately is often missing since it is not attached and simply sits around the inner works. The lamps don't do very much without the outer sleeve, so one should be made if an original is not available. Many different themes and color patterns exist. Themes shown include the American Flag (which is also shown without the outer sleeve), small flowers, fish, butterflies, large flowers, and colored blobs. (With the exception of the colored blobs model, the ones shown are less psychedelic in performance than most lamps in this section.) A variation on this idea is a self-contained lamp that sits on a black plastic base, has its own top, and features color patterns. $100.00 – 150.00 with sleeve.

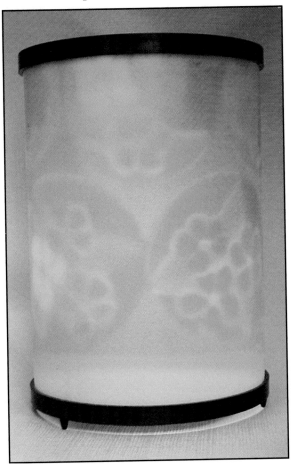

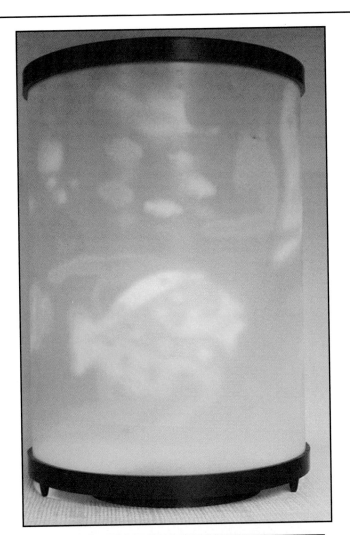

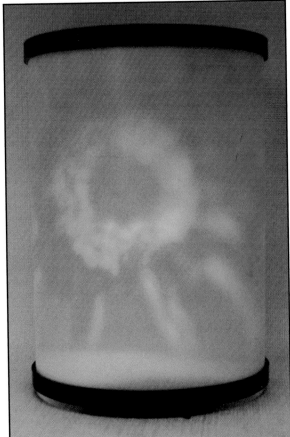

❖ Advertising Lamps ❖

As far back as the 1920s when electric motion lamps first appeared, their use as a means for advertising was established. With early large and sturdy Scene-in-Action specialty lamps paving the path for the later Econo-lite Motion-in-Advertising models and the Goodman 3-D Displays, advertisers found they could relay their messages in an eye-catching, effective manner. The use of animation in advertising continued throughout the 1960s and 1970s up to the present. By far the most frequent employers of such advertising were beer and liquor companies. Even with integrated circuits and motorized devices at their disposal, the simplicity, low cost, and low maintenance of advertising motion lamps have had quite an appeal to manufacturers.

The use of colored moving blips (where the action imitates the motion of a heartbeat monitor) and the "glimmer/glisten" style of animation (where dots outlining images or words sparkle) were frequent. The wide variety of designs and styles of these lamps make them alluring to collectors of motion lamps as well as to collectors of advertising. Small or large, wall mount or shelf mount, simple or complex, the end result is the same. Advertisers want you to notice their products and hopefully use them. As aficionados, we have noticed their lamps — and while we may not always use the corresponding products — we certainly want to use the lamps!

Note that most of these lamps were not sold to the general public, making them harder to find than many mass-produced lamps. However, with some searching you will see that many have gotten into circulation rather than being discarded when no longer needed by store owners. We have not included comments about degree of rarity for this section since it is a factor that is much harder to determine with these. However, we have still assigned values based on the most popular ones we have handled and seen on the market.

Liquor advertising lamps appear first, followed by varied other advertising units grouped by theme.

"ABC Supreme Beer" (1940s)

Water falls while cabin chimney smokes.

A sizeable unit that catches the eye. $200.00 – 250.00.

"Ancient Age Bourbon" (1950s)

The shade spins.

Simple advertising piece for Kentucky bourbon. The base is not original, and it is even possible that the shade had a fan added by someone long ago to make it spin! $50.00 – 75.00.

"Bacardi Rum" (1960s?)

Latin men and women are dancing under twinkling stars as words below change color.

More colorful than most, this one is quite attractive. $100.00 – 125.00.

"Bellows Whiskey" (1950s)

Windows light and change color and product name is highlighted.

The extruded plastic front makes this unit better than average. Designed to hold a bottle of the product on each side in cups provided. $150.00 – 175.00.

"Budweiser Lager Beer" (1950s?)
The shade spins around.

A lamp that is shaped like a can of beer and has a typical label transcribed onto the surface. The sides say "take home 6." It is designed for wall mounting. $75.00 – 125.00.

"Budweiser" (1970s)
The product label glistens and words at bottom change color.

This popular beer company, with the Visual Effects Co., produced a motion lamp that is quite effective with its busy animation. $75.00 – 100.00.

"Budweiser" (1993)

This lamp is exactly like the one above at right but it is smaller in size. It was made in China and marked copyright by Anheuser Busch. They were commonly sold in Spencer Gift stores for $19.95. We have heard that the lamp was not authorized by the brewery but cannot confirm this. $25.00 – 35.00 especially if mint in the box.

"Calvert Extra" (1970s)

Color blips move at top and bottom while words change color.

This model is designed to sit on top of a bottle of the product. $75.00 – 100.00.

"Calvert Extra" (1970s?)

Similar to photo at left with somewhat different graphics. It is always nice to find matching bottles with units of this style, but we seldom find them that way. One can usually find suitable bottles at a later date, so don't pass up good lamps because the bottles are gone. $75.00 – 100.00.

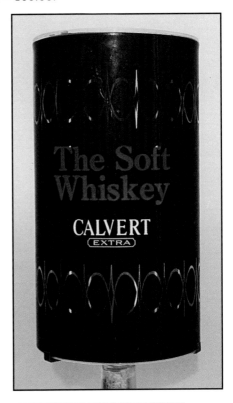

"Canadian Lord Calvert" (1960s?)

Color blips appear at top and bottom while images and words change color.

Another lamp designed to sit on top of a bottle. $75.00 – 100.00.

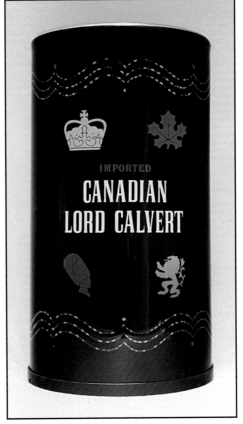

"Lord Calvert" (1970s?)

The product label and company name glimmer on one side while a "twister" whirls on the other side with glimmering words.

This is a fascinating lamp and is not the standard liquor advertising piece since both sides are totally different. $100.00 – 125.00.

"Cook's '500' Ale" (1950s)

The shade spins around.

Typical of the label style, this lamp says "take home 6" on the sides and is a wall mount model $75.00 – 125.00.

"Cook's Goldblume Beer" (1950s?)

The shade spins around.

Shaped like a beer can, this one says "take home 6" on the sides and is designed for wall mounting. A simple table mount base also exists. Produced by Hal Mfg. Co. of Ohio. $75.00 – 125.00.

"Coors Display Lamp" (1960s?)

The large shade spins as words and symbols glimmer. A waterfall in black and white runs on one side while a waterfall in color runs on the other side

This unit can be shelf-mounted or wall mounted and it is effective since the ad line "brewed with pure Rocky Mountain water" is visually enhanced by the waterfalls. A large, finely swirled cylinder inside produces the animation. $125.00 – 175.00.

"Dickel Whiskey" (1960s)

Color blips move at top and bottom while product name glimmers and changes colors.

A dazzling lamp that is designed to be mounted on top of bottle or placed on a shelf. The larger manufacturers should take note of this one! $100.00 – 125.00.

"Falstaff Beer" (1960s)

A beer mug bubbles and glistens.

Produced by Thomas A. Schutz Co. of Morton Grove, Illinois, the lamp has a paper scene glued onto a plastic framework with a metal back. It uses an unusual perforated metal cylinder for the light effects. $150.00 – 200.00.

"Genesee Cream Ale" (1960s?)

Patterns weave in a psychedelic manner as the product name is highlighted and the words "cream ale" appear and disappear.

This company used motion advertising more than most and this is a nice example. $75.00 – 100.00.

"Genesee Beer" (1950s)

The company name glimmers as does the wording while the shade spins around.

An inner blue and white striped sleeve produces the effects in this wall-mount lamp. A variation of this model sits on a shelf. Made by Plascolite Company. $75.00 – 125.00.

"Genesee Beer" (1970s)

Colorful swirls dance around the company name.

Marked Coronet of NY and Genesee Brewing Co. of NY, this lamp is similar to a standard psychedelic lamp in size and action. $75.00 – 100.00.

"Genesee Beer and Ale" (1950s)

Letters of the company name sparkle as the shade spins around.

This unit looks like a small table lamp and has an inner blue and white striped sleeve to produce the animation effects. A variation has a different "B" side that reads "Always ask for Jenny." $75.00 – 100.00.

"Genesee Beer/Cream Ale" (1960s?)

Colors project onto an open window area.

There are two bulbs on top of one another that drive the cylinder. The sizeable unit is designed for wall mounting. It is gold colored while a variation for cream ale is green and black, differs graphically, and has different coloring on the cylinder. $125.00 – 150.00.

"Hamm's Beer" (1963)

An inside cylinder with a scene spins one way while the outer shade with product information spins the other way. The company name alternates with two window openings that show a scene of a pretty tree-lined coastal area.

It can be wall- or shelf-mounted by adjusting the pivot arm. A harder-to-find variation has an inner scene of a black man and woman having dinner at a table. Sometimes getting just one cylinder to spin is a challenge, so these dual cylinder lamps can really be fun if clearance is tight! Produced by Embossograph Co. of Chicago, Illinois. $100.00 – 125.00.

"Golden Grain Belt Beer" (1950s?)

Images on graphic glisten while words on cylinder project through.

An interesting frame holds the motion unit and is marked Minneapolis Brewing Co. $150.00 – 175.00.

"Hamm's Lampshade" (1950s?)

Product name and water below sparkle.

Wording reads "the beer refreshing. . . from the land of sky blue waters." An inner animation sleeve produces the sparkle effect. Originally sat on a plastic base similar to the Goodman Circus lamp. It is possible it may have been a Goodman product. $125.00 – 150.00 with proper base.

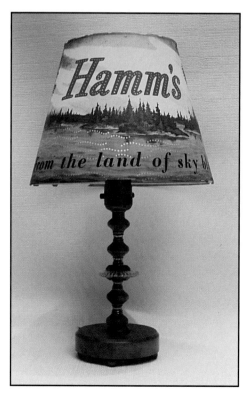

"Hamm's Beer Molded Lamp" (1960s?)

Ice glistens and sparkles.

Words project through. A three-dimensional lamp produced by L.A. Goodman. $150.00 – 200.00.

"Heileman's Old Style Beer" (1950s?)

Beer foams on the face of a large mug.

This one is sizeable and an impressive figural display. It is designed for wall mounting. The cylinder and an inner sleeve produce the foaming effect. $175.00 – 225.00.

"Heileman's Old Style Green Tankard" (1950s)

Inner cylinder with graphics spins.

The tankard has a window opening highlighting the cylinder inside that reads "Heileman's Old Style Lager — aged longer than any other beer." A man and a woman in period costume flank a mug of beer as well. Designed to be used on a shelf and produced by Thomas A. Schutz Co. of Chicago. $150.00 – 175.00.

"Imperial Hiram Walker Whiskey" (1950s)

Words go by a caption area that stems from the mouths of a singing barbershop quartet.

A fragile but nifty design on a small lamp that is hard to find without some warping. It is often missing the red top that includes two clips to hold a cardboard sign that reads "I'm the Man." This lamp was produced by L.A. Goodman. It is sometimes damaged today because the tiny lamp was originally supplied with a 60-watt bulb!.$125.00 – 175.00.

"Johnnie Walker Black Label" (1970s)

Color blips move at top and bottom while words appear one by one and read from top to bottom; all words go black and then the phrase "12 Year Old" appears.

A simple but very effective lamp. $100.00 – 125.00.

"Johnnie Walker Red" (1970s)

Color blips move at top and bottom while words and product name change color.

The figure of Johnnie on the lamp is nice but unfortunately is not animated. We know they could have done better with this lamp. $75.00 – 100.00.

"Kentucky Gentleman Bourbon" (1960s?)

Words change color, color blips move, and the small Kentucky Gentleman images below change color.

An attractive and active-looking lamp designed to sit on a bottle of the product; this one is simple but quite eye-catching. $100.00 – 125.00.

"Kessler" (1960s?)

Words change color as color bars flash.

The activity of the animation demands your attention. $75.00 – 100.00.

"Mateus White Rosé Wine" (1960s?)

Wording changes color while color blips move.

Features dual color blip patterns at top and bottom. $75.00 – 100.00.

"Miller Beer Bottle on Ice Bucket" (1960s)

The company name and wording change colors as the plastic "ice" above glows.

Produced by Thomas Schutz of Illinois, this smart design is fetching and a good figural piece. $125.00 – 150.00.

"Molson – Imported From Canada" (1950s?)

The shade spins as dots sparkle and the product name glistens.

A tiny beer keg acts as the base, making this a cute one. It features a train on one side and a steamboat on the other, since both vehicles credit John Molson with introducing steam travel to Canada. The animation is produced by an inner color-striped sleeve. $100.00 – 125.00.

"Mouquin Brandy" (1970s)

The shade spins around.

This unit is simply designed and can be mounted on a product bottle. It has actual photos on the shade. $50.00 – 75.00.

"Nikolai Vodka" (1960s?)

Wording changes color while color blips move.

The product known as the "caviar of vodkas" is featured here. $75.00 – 100.00.

"Old Smuggler Scotch" (Animated) (1950s?)

Wording "careful, don't waste a drop" appears, then drops of product drip into the cup as product name below flashes and changes color.

Prominent attractive graphic with Scottish man in kilt. Designed to sit on top of bottle. Unique use of dripping liquor makes it a standout. $100.00 – 125.00.

"Old Smuggler Scotch" (1950s?)

The shade spins around.

The product name and images are highlighted on a motion unit that sits on a bottle. $50.00 – 75.00.

"Old Export Beer" (1950s)

The product name glistens.

A lamp which highlights a Maryland-made beer. An alternate style features a small metal pedestal base. $75.00 – 125.00.

"Oertels 92 Lager Beer" (1950s)

The label on the large bottle glimmers as words project onto it and pass by.

This is quite an impressive advertising piece with its bottle framework in plastic and its fine animation. The bottle lifts off the metal base to expose the cylinder. Harder to find than most. $250.00 – 300.00.

"Ortlieb's Premium Lager Beer" (1950s)

Letters of the company name sparkle as the shade spins around.

Shaped like a large beer can, the inner column of blue and white swirled plastic provides the animation. $100.00 – 125.00.

"Pabst Blue Ribbon Christmas Tree Display" (1950s)

Wording and ornaments on the tree change color and glow while product bottle glows, and three colored prisms representing snow flakes sparkle.

Paper, cardboard, and styrofoam construction is used in a unit that required assembly. With a size of about 15" x 17", it is a winsome piece that also serves as a crossover collectible. The bottle here is updated. $175.00 – 225.00.

"Pabst Blue Ribbon" (1960s?)

The cylinder reflects patterns on the shade.

Produced by Embossograph Display Mfg. Co., the lamp has an interesting shape with the company name on the front and the logo on the sides of an antique style lamp shade. $75.00 – 125.00.

"P.M. Whiskey" (1950s?)
Colors shift behind the graphic.

Marked National Distilling Products Corp., N.Y. Probably meant to be placed near a display of the product which would give you "pleasing moments." $150.00 – 175.00.

"Riunite Wine" (1981 & 1982)
The company name and words change as small color blips move at top and bottom while the product is shown sitting on sparkling ice.

Copyrighted by Villa Banfi of Farmingdale, N.Y., the inner cylinder spins so that words can be read as they change color. The 1981 version features lovers in a gondola drinking the product as the river flows via the turning cylinder. $100.00 – 125.00.

"Rolling Rock Premium Beer" (1950s)

Colors radiate from spring water area by horse.

Extruded plastic construction has similarities to the Goodman 3-D displays, and it may just be one of those. In any event, it is quite attractive and effective. $175.00 – 225.00.

"Seagram's 7" (1970s)

The famous red 7 and gold crown glow and sparkle while fringe around the company name comes and goes.

An impressive looking advertising piece, due chiefly to the large glowing 7. Made by the Visual Effects Co. $100.00 – 125.00.

"Royal 58 Beer" (1950s)

Words glisten.

Styled like a miniature table lamp, the rear reads "make a date with 58." $100.00 – 125.00.

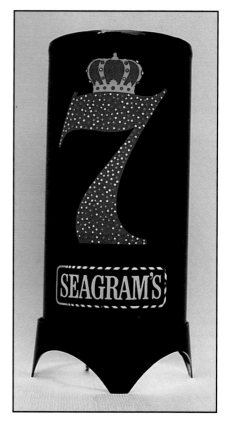

"Seagram's 7 Crown Whiskey" (1940s?)

Product name glimmers as cylinder spins by a small window in lower portion of the label with words traveling across.

A cute design featuring a realistic mini bottle of the product that is made of a celluloid type plastic. $150.00 – 200.00.

"Stoney's Pilsener Beer" (1950s)

The shade revolves while the company name glimmers.

An inner striped cylinder is used for animation. Both sides are identical. $100.00 – 125.00.

"St. Pauli Girl Beer" (1983)

Color blips move at top and bottom while words change color.

Good advertising lamp with attractive graphics and a late production date. $100.00 – 125.00.

"Taylor Gin" (1970s)

The shade spins around.

Designed to be mounted above a product bottle, the map of the world emphasizes their words "finest gin the world around." $50.00 – 75.00.

"Wacker's Bohemian Pale Beer" (1950s)
Words glisten.

Advertising piece for a beer from Lancaster, Penna. $100.00 – 125.00.

"Wild Turkey Bourbon" (1960s?)
The shade spins around.

Pictures of turkeys on the shade and the wording convey product message in a very simple lamp. $50.00 – 75.00.

"Anson Lindé Stars" (1960s?)

Stars in the skyline sparkle as do sapphire images on the shade. Words
change color while city scene below changes from night to day.

Used to promote star sapphires in jewelry stores, this is an unusual lamp with a large base of wire metal to support examples of the product. $125.00 – 150.00.

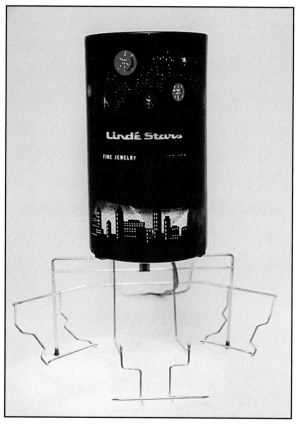

"Copley Diamonds" (1940s?)

Wording glows with subtle color shifts.

Using wood construction with chromed metal trim and plastic lettering set into a heavy cardboard graphic, the unknown manufacturer creates an effect similar to the glow of a neon tube sign. An outer plastic window covers the graphic and the red, blue, and clear plastic lettering pieces pass through the cardboard and add depth to the look. Unfortunately, the actual product is somewhat hard to see. $200.00 – 225.00.

"Bisma-Rex" (1940s?)
The shade spins around.

An antacid product is advertised in this lamp featuring very sturdy construction. $100.00 – 150.00.

"Ko-Pak-Ta Toasted Peanuts" (1930s)
Flames dance around graphic.

The vibrant scene of black pygmies dancing near a cauldron enhances the animation. Designed to hold peanuts above the animation unit, the heat of the bulb would also keep the product warm. It is chrome plated and somewhat prone to pitting at this age. It contains a standard cylinder and animation sleeve for the effects. Be sure that the peanut tray is included, as it keeps light focused on the large animation area. (See More Motion Sickness chapter for a variation of this model.) $350.00 – 400.00.

"Fireside Toasted Peanuts" (1930s)

Flames dance around graphic.

Very similar to the preceding lamp, but with red and black devils dancing and a different animation unit inside similar to the Gritt system. The case is brushed aluminum which tends to be in better condition. $350.00 – 400.00.

"D-Lux Nuts" (1950s)

Circus animals and figures spin around.

A colorful and fairly large unit that doubles as a holding compartment and warmer for peanuts. The top says "Lift the Big Top, Get 'Em Hot." With a nice unit like this, who could avoid buying peanuts? A variation of this has different colors on upper half showing a clown and different wording. The title reads "BIG TOP CIRCUS NUTS." Note: A group of mint in the box examples was released onto the market some years ago, but these lamps are still far from plentiful. Curiously, the company name that the elephant on the cylinder carries on its side is often purposely blacked out. $350.00 – 400.00.

"Clock of Tomorrow" (1950s)
The shade spins around.

Images and model numbers of clocks appear on the shade, focusing attention on the product designed to sit underneath. Cheaply made with cardboard construction. Produced by General Time Corporation. $40.00 – 60.00.

"Westclox Clock of Tomorrow" (1950s?)
Atom and star designs sparkle and change color.

The shade is suspended over a color-striped animation sleeve. The metal wire base is shaped like a sawhorse with four legs. $125.00 – 150.00.

"Caravelle Watches" (1960s?)
Cylinder with advertising spins inside window opening.

The surrounding framework allows products to be displayed. An eye stopper to grace sales counters. $125.00 – 150.00.

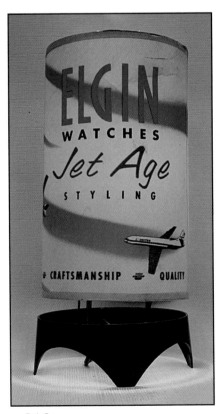

"Elgin Watches" (1950s?)
The shade revolves.

The fact that Elgin watches had Jet Age styling is enhanced by United Airlines jet planes flying about. This is not the correct base for this lamp. $75.00 – 125.00.

"Wakmann Watches" (1950s)

Words glisten while raindrops and wreath outline gleam.

Shaped exactly like the Genesee beer lamp but even more interesting since it has raindrops and also a rear side that features a Christmas theme. $125.00 – 150.00.

"Brach's Halloween Candies" (1950s?)

A witch, devil, and an owl pass in silhouette on the moon.

Uses cardboard and paper construction. Quite winsome and a crossover collectible. $225.00 – 300.00.

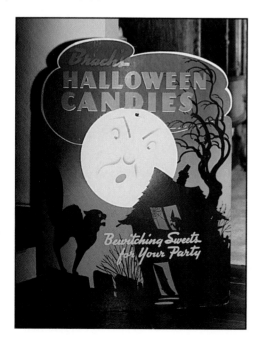

"Hoffmans Ice Cream" (1920s)

Colors shift behind the ad graphics.

A beautiful wood frame holds the textured glass along with a plastic lithograph of a lady on it beside the words, "Always Hoffmans Superior Ice Cream." Definitely eye catching. $350.00 – 500.00.

"Lufthansa Airlines" (1960s)
Airplanes fly as the world beneath revolves.

A unique and stylish designer lamp with its large metal boomerang-shaped aluminum piece intersecting the V-shaped wood base. The shade is asymmetrical, or teardrop-shaped, which is very unusual for a motion lamp. The cylinder has the whole world on it in color and provides a simple but very effective animation. It was made overseas and is truly a great lamp. Our collector friend Paul Miller is a retired airline pilot who conjectured that the boomerang piece signifies how the airline always returns to its original departure site while the V-shaped base signifies the swept-back wings of a jet plane. If true, this would be one very significant lamp design. $500.00 – 700.00.

"Luminite Display Products Co." (1930s)
A colored cylinder casts shadows on the graphic.

The rugged metal framework supports glass behind which a company's advertising or message could be inserted and enhanced by the motion. $100.00 – 125.00 and more with famous ads.

"O-Cedar Polish" (1930s?)
Colors shift onto the globe.

Made by the Commercial Utilities Mfg. Co. of Chicago, the large glass sphere sits on a metal base. An unusual lamp that curiously leaves little space for air flow. $150.00 – 200.00.

"Old Glory Display" (1940s?)
The American flag appears to wave in the breeze.

The very large wood and glass framework is backed with a heavy cardboard body and top. The cylinder, possibly not original, is made of plastic with fibers running through it and has a black striped pattern painted on. The effect is not entirely successful, but it is the only flag lamp we have seen. It was used to advertise flags for a company selling them, and had a matching unit that could sit on either side to advertise fireworks as well. Very scarce. $250.00 – 350.00.

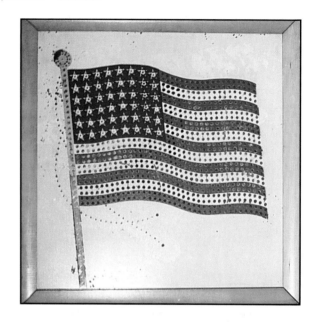

"Pennzoil" (1954)
The product name glistens.

Made by Plascolite Display Signs of Los Angeles, Calif. It has a striped inner sleeve for the animation effects. $125.00 – 150.00.

"Phillips 66 Trop-Artic Motor Oil" (1960s?)

The shade spins around.

Set on a tripod base, it probably sold more motor oil than a static sign would have sold. $100.00 – 125.00.

"Sinclair Motor Oil" (1950s)

Words glisten as do red stripes.

Another cylinder with colored stripes produces the animation. $125.00 – 150.00.

"General Electric 'VIR' Broadcast Controlled Color TV" (1960s)

Color blips near the center move.

Inner colored bar cylinder produces animation that is rather limited for this prominent company. $100.00 – 125.00.

"Raytheon TV Tubes and Service" (1950s)

Products glimmer and words projecting from cylinder pass by the upper and lower borders.

An excellent advertising piece with its attractive graphics. It is somewhat prone to image flaking and is harder to find than most. $175.00 – 250.00.

"Rusling Wood" (1940s)

Spinning cylinder casts off colors.

All we have of this piece is a marked metal stand and cylinder. We suspect it may have been used behind logs to give a fire-like effect. If complete, value may be $75.00 – 100.00.

"Seneca County Fair" (1950s?)

The shade revolves.

A fair held in Tiffin, Ohio, is the subject of this advertising piece. $50.00 – 75.00.

"7-UP the Uncola" (1970s)
The product name glistens along with the product label.

A good advertising unit that is basically an Op Lamp made by Creative Lighting Co. The white sparkle is similar to the fizz of the product which is very fitting. $125.00 – 150.00.

"Taperlite Candles" (1940s)
Candle tips burn and flicker.

Good-sized unit with a unique theme found in few lamps, that of candles burning. Advertises a product touted as "hand dips, odorless, dripless." The manufacturer of the candles was Willow-Kaumer Candle Co. of Syracuse, N.Y. They called themselves the "world's leading candle manufacturers since 1855." $250.00 – 300.00.

"United Cigars" (1930s?)
Colors shift.

The large glass, metal, and wood framework is sturdy. It appears to be made by the same company as the Hoffmans Ice Cream lamp. $300.00 – 400.00.

"Whistleswitch Remote Control" (1970s?)

Dots glisten around the wording.

The graphic features a small TV screen with football players. Unusual lamp with limited animation. $100.00 – 125.00.

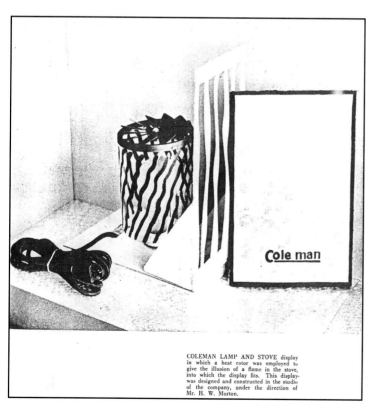

COLEMAN LAMP AND STOVE display in which a heat rotor was employed to give the illusion of a flame in the stove, into which the display fits. This display was designed and constructed in the studio of the company, under the direction of Mr. H. W. Morton.

Cylinder Action Displays

Have a Record of Achievement — With the Surface Merely Scratched

By EDWIN L. ROSS, General Manager, Fischer Action Displays Division
Fischer Exhibits, Inc., New York

AMONG action displays it is my opinion that cylinder action, which permits the development of so many life-like illusions, has stood the test of successful experience in the seventeen years that it has been on the market, as no worth-while substitute has been found for cylinder action in the simulation of fire, running liquids and various other sales-bearing illusions and messages.

Also, experience justifies the conviction that this style of action display has greater possibilities at the present time than it has had in the past. Today we have not only our accumulated experience to guide us, but also the advantages of new materials, improved technical skill and better lighting elements. As a result, the man who has been trained to design striking action-illusion effects is now in a position to improve the art and technique of the past. We are likewise more familiar with the problems of distribution and we know how to better insure maximum showings.

Some people think the revolving cylinder in this kind of display is the whole story, but that is not entirely true. It is rather the combination of the design on the revolving cylinder with the design on the intervening shield or screen, which crystallizes action and brings out excellent illusions. At one time, as a result of failure to understand basic principles, the motion was limited to one direction only. But now, using only one cylinder and one bulb, we are able to establish motion running in various directions, all perfectly timed. New special lacquers are also very efficient in bringing out life-like and colorful effects, while more depths and more planes have added much to this type of action display.

An example of this new development is seen in the fairly recent display in which three different kinds of liquor seemingly flow through the air into three cocktail glasses. It has received very favorable comment because it is still being continuously used after two years. On the same principle we can take any combustion engine and cross-section it to show every working part in action — and this result is accomplished by means of cylinder, shield and heat unit only. Such action as waterfalls, fire scenes and an infinite variety of color effects may seem to be difficult, but in reality are very simple when compared with the multiple actions we now successfully handle.

Excellent art work and knowledge of the right transparency to use in each given case are vital elements, and when deftly employed to visualize a sound selling theme are, in my opinion, superior to any other form of display merchandising, because they stop and interest so many more people. Still further, the cost of this type of display is now much lower in price; about one-half of former years. A situation which is due to improved production methods and the expiration of patents, thus reducing production costs and eliminating royalties.

We are now able to show life-like illusions of airplanes passing through the clouds, with traveling smoke letters, or a message spelled out through the exhaust. Automobiles scurrying along the road, with scenery passing by, are now possible, as well as liquors and soft drinks in thirst-appealing action, as well as new heating units showing every moving part in natural colors. Action displays of this character have been created for paint and varnish makers, for proprietary medicines, radios, transportation and other lines of merchandise and service. In fact, it is now possible to put into action, or surround with action, almost anything saleable. Naturally, I lean toward cylinder action displays, as my experience has been chiefly with them. As a result of those years of fascinating work in creating and selling such displays, it is my firm belief that the cylinder action display, which has accomplished so much for advertisers in the past, is capable of doing still more for them in the future.

However, like anything worth-while, good judgment must be applied — not only in selecting, but in handling and installation. Performance is vital and so there is no alibi for placing this kind of display in either an over-heated or sub-zero window without proper circulation of air through vent holes in the platform, correct angle of rotor blades and correctly proportioned vents on the lid. Jewel bearings, hardened steel points and suitable lamp bulbs are additional important elements necessary to secure perfect performance under all circumstances.

These things are very simple and fundamental for the man with experience and training to know what it is all about, but when the novice has tackled the cylinder action display he has too often overlooked some essential element, and thus brought a bad name on this branch of the display industry. That is, of course, an unfortunate feature of every business which calls for experience and skill, and is particularly so when the article has the seeming of being so easy to make, as does the cylinder action display.

Further, while some types of motion displays may be safely packed and shipped in sections for assembly by the dealer, that does not apply to the cylinder action display. It must be sent out complete for installation, unless it is to be installed by a professional window display service, as expert assembly is a prime requirement if satisfactory results are to be secured. Simple though it may be, the dealer or clerk is rare who can fully understand printed directions — something the best of inexperienced folks can seldom do.

JOHNS MANVILLE FIREPROOF ROOF. This display is in a metal shadow box, size 30x40. In natural colors this was an outstanding display as it visualized in simulated flame effect how burning brands from one house might alight on a J.M. roof and roll off without damage.

ALEMITE GAS-co-lator in action showing the course of dirty gasoline through the strainer and thence out when cleaned for use.

KENNEDY STOKING SYSTEM. Large metal and glass display shows in action large lumps of coal dropping from hopper into pulverizing cylinder from whence powdered coal is blown into the combustion chamber of the furnace.

U. S. RUBBER COMPANY instruction sheet sent to all dealers receiving this heat motor display.

Reprinted from "Display Animation 1938"
(Reeder-Morton Publications)

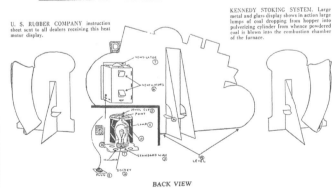

BACK VIEW

IMPORTANT INSTRUCTIONS
FOR SETTING UP ACTION DISPLAY NO. T 3461

Follow numbers on drawing for assembling —

After opening the two packages, set the lithograph cut-out on a level floor and place the easel (a) in position to allow the display to stand up. Now take out of the small package the standard wire (3) the socket (2) the lamp (11) and the revolving cylinder (10) and get ready to assemble the display.

Place the standard wire (3) under the upper part of the socket, as shown in drawing, and screw to the lower part of the socket through the middle hole on the card board marked (b) so that it is in position as shown in drawing (c). Screw the bulb in the socket, now insert the card board (b) slots into side pieces as shown in box of drawing (d). When every slot has been placed in position and the box is securely assembled place the cylinder (10) so that the jewel cut (5) is resting on point (4). Care should be taken to see that the cylinder (10) clears all sides and is not touching in any place. Now close the top through slots provided and open ventilator (7). Now you are ready to put the display to operate, by plugging on any 115 volts current, either AC or DC. The display will start to operate as soon as enough heat has concentrated inside of the cylinder.

If the window in which the display is placed is so close as to contain stagnated air, open the extra ventilators (6) as shown in drawing.

[167]

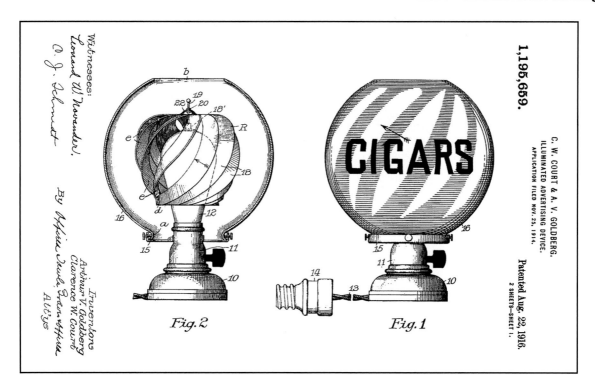

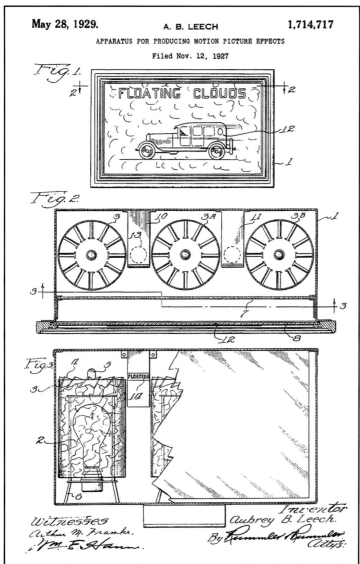

More U.S. patent application drawings.

❦ Maintenance and Troubleshooting ❦

Motion lamps are relatively simple and usually work fine, but problems can develop. Based on years of examining, operating, and trial and error-ing with motion lamps, we offer our helpful tips.

Bulb Selection

Bulb wattage

The most commonly made mistake is using bulbs with high wattage. Manufacturers recommended 20-to-60 watt bulbs. Never use bulbs with wattage exceeding 60 in standard motion lamps. In fact, even when original instructions specify 60-watt, use 40-watt bulbs. They will burn cooler and protect our aging lamps from deterioration while not sacrificing performance. Most Scene-in-Action lamps used 20-watt bulbs which produce less heat and burn longer than the higher wattage bulbs found in most later lamps. For this reason, it is not uncommon to find the interiors of these now over 65 year-old lamps in good condition. If 20-watt bulbs are not available, 25-watt bulbs will be fine. Some Scene-in-Action specialty lamps that were used commercially often contained 100-watt partially frosted bulbs, but even in these, a lower wattage would be advisable. All Rev-o-lite, National, and Roto-Vue, Jr. lamps work well with 25-watt bulbs.

Bulb type

Always use clear glass bulbs in motion lamps. The light projection from these is pure and sharp. Using frosted or colored glass will result in diffused light that will muddy the animation or even eliminate it entirely. We have advised many dealers to use clear bulbs as a sales aid. A few have followed our advice, but most have not bothered and continue to offer lamps as found with frosted bulbs. Frosted bulbs severely decrease market appeal, folks! And dealers take note: lamps will sell much faster when they are lit. These are, after all, motion lamps and the motion can only be seen when lit. But for heaven's sake, leave them off if you haven't bothered to put in the proper wattage bulbs. Don't add injury to insult. Note that certain lamps will look fine with a frosted bulb, in fact some may even look better since there will be no "hot spots" seen. Some psychedelic lamps, children's lamps, simple non-animated revolving shade lamps, and a few others fall into this category. As with anything subjective, select the look that pleases you most.

Bulb filament shape and height

There are circular, straight vertical, straight horizontal, pointed, and other bulb filament shapes. We urge collectors to experiment with these different styles for the best results and satisfaction. A circular filament yields a softer, often more natural image. A straight filament yields a sharper, bolder, but sometimes harsh image. Personal taste comes into play here. For example, we prefer a straight horizontal filament in an Econolite Train lamp. The resulting animation is rich and well-defined without looking harsh or phony. However, using the same bulb in the Historical Fires lamp results in having the animation sleeve images appear static, not moving. A circular filament is a much more appropriate choice here. (Most Econolite lamps were originally supplied with a V-shaped filament.) Also, turning the outer shade left or right will result in different projection angles from the bulb. Some angles will give a more satisfying look than others, so try adjusting the shades.

Filament height is also a factor, a rather subtle one that is usually ignored. We have discovered that the filament height will alter the alignment of the animation somewhat. Just an inch or two up or down can change the light patterns enough so that a lighthouse beacon will appear to emanate from the stone structure below rather than the glass windows. Again, experiment for the best results. Also watch for the size of a bulb's glass envelope. A slender bulb keeps its distance and will not touch the delicate cylinder walls. A fat bulb can come dangerously close to melting the plastic and also may rub against the cylinder.

Three bulb filaments used in motion lamps.

Cylinders That Will Not Spin

After the power is turned on, a lamp should start working within one to two minutes. A gentle turn with a finger should help start a cold lamp, but it may not continue to spin. If that is the case, read on.

Static electricity

The number one adversary of a motion lamp is static electricity. Even a sane person can go crazy trying to tame this invisible gremlin! Static can come and go with variations in the weather, especially humidity changes. Colder and drier air will carry static electricity easier than warmer, wetter air. If a cylinder will not spin in a balanced and unwarped lamp, do the following. Lift off the shade and moisten both cylinder surfaces and then the animation sleeve with a soft, water dampened cloth. Then make sure you do not dry it. Drying will bring static right back. Rubbing the surfaces with a clothes dryer anti-static sheet will also work but can leave a residue and   sometimes an odor. Static spray will also work, but our preference is still a water-dampened cloth.

Defective pivot cups

The majority of motion lamps use a metal cup that is jeweled. Dropping a cylinder roughly onto a steel pivot can crack the jewel which is often a sapphire. When this happens, the cylinder will not spin and the naked eye cannot usually see the problem. Switching one cylinder for another the same size (as long as both are static free) will point out a defective pivot cup. Try spinning the cylinder with the shade off to eliminate any obstructions. Glass cups or bearings are used by many motion lamps instead of jewel cups. Those that are cracked can be seen upon examination. Modern lamps use plastic cups, which will wear out sooner and are not as friction free, but seem to be less problem prone. In any type, a drop or two of lightweight oil (like sewing machine oil) placed in the cup will prevent rust and lessen friction.

Dull pivot points

Our favorite pivot point is found on an Econolite. It looks like a fat steel phonograph needle. It is sturdy and will not prick your finger like a thinner one will. Suspending it with a tightly coiled spring, the manufacturer allowed this type of point to flex and not break off easily. Soldered-on pivot points are more prone to snapping off, and some manufacturers simply sharpened the ends of the pivot rods to form points. In any style, all points should be sharp. If they are not, gentle filing will sharpen them. Remember that only a mild current of rising hot air drives motion lamps, so it is easy to see how the slightest bit of resistance can and will stop them from working. We caution all people handling lamps to be very careful when placing a cylinder on a pivot point or removing it. Not watching what you are doing may result in cylinders that are scratched by the sharp pivot points. This sort of damage is seldom repairable and will almost certainly show when the lamp is operating.

Warping

Examine the inner sleeve or space in which the cylinder must spin. If the sleeve is warped toward the cylinder because of age or heat, it will not have enough room to clear and will jam. Holding a lamp level above your head will often allow you to see this problem. Or turn the shade upside down and place the cylinder inside to detect areas that could rub.

Curing warpage can be one of the most difficult challenges a lamp collector may face. Heat probably caused the problem to begin with and heat is the only cure. Careful heating is one method that works if you protect your fingers and try to reshape while the piece is flexible. Complete removal of the offending part for heating is tricky and not recommended for beginners. Either way, results may be temporary as distorted plastic seems to have a memory and may return to its previous shape a day or even a week later. As heat could also cause further damage, proceed with extreme caution.

A badly warped inner sleeve.

Pivot rod centering

A pivot rod will usually flex in any direction. The goal is to center the rod to allow the cylinder to clear the animation sleeve or any other obstructions. In the case of a round Scene-in-Action lamp, the cylinder has very little space in which to rotate and any plastic shrinkage in the animation sleeve will reduce the space even further, allowing only a fraction of an inch for clearance. Here, centering is critical and may take some patience. Also very important is the height of the rod. With shrinkage, alignment will change. Again using Scene-in-Action as an example, consider the Colonial Fountain. The cylinder was designed to create the effect of water at the very top of the fountain flowing up and down with varying pressure. If the cylinder is out of alignment with the animation glass, this neat effect will not be seen. Adjusting the rod up or down with careful bending will correct it.

Lamps that won't light

After trying a new bulb, your choices will be narrowed to a bad plug, cord, lamp socket, or switch. Test offenders one at a time until the culprit is found. All of these parts are readily available at most good hardware or electrical supply stores.

Air flow and heat dissipation

If your collection is crammed into tight spaces or if many lamps are grouped closely together, we recommend you check the air flow for best performance. Check the heat level especially if you are using high wattage bulbs. Damage may occur slowly without your knowing it. This is even more important if the lamps are left burning for long periods of time. We certainly want to avoid distorting lamps in perfect shape.

Cylinder speed

Cylinder speed is a very simple factor that can dramatically affect animation. If the fan blades are opened wider, the cylinder speed will increase. If the blades are closed tighter, the cylinder speed will decrease. A higher wattage bulb will increase the heat and thereby the speed. More often than not, more speed is needed. But if you want to slow the cylinder down, add a bit of weight to it. You can do this by affixing a washer or two to the fan, but remember that good balance is necessary. We have a Coors beer lamp that has poor animation unless it runs at a nice slow speed to show the waterfall and other effects. Usually the manufacturer has taken cylinder speed into account when designing the size and shape. But as variation with age occurs, making adjustments will compensate.

Cylinder interchange

Cylinders made by the same company can often be interchanged successfully. For example, many cylinders made for round lamps will work in corresponding oval lamps, but not always. The Econolite Forest Fire cylinder supplied with a round lamp has a slightly different pattern on the lower portion than their oval lamp cylinder. Putting the round lamp cylinder into an oval Econolite Forest Fire will result in improper water flow. Sometimes the cylinder graphics are printed in reverse between oval and round lamps and they may also spin in different directions. Here switching would be useless. To go even further, Goodman oval lamp cylinders are often a different size and color from their corresponding round lamp cousins, so don't even think of switching. The rule of thumb for interchanging cylinders is test before switching. Of course, any cylinder that will fit into a lamp lacking one will yield some action. The action may very well be wrong or poor, but at least it will resemble motion.

Lamp bases

Any Scene-in-Action round bases can be used on any of their various round lamps. Most Econolite Roto-Vue, Jr. bases can be interchanged by unscrewing the scene sleeves, although there are color differences that may or may not match the scene. All Econolite full-size round or oval shades will fit their respective chain-link design bases with the familiar three black painted wooden balls. Height of pivot rods may vary and need to be adjusted. Pedestal bases are fairly standard with both Econolite and Goodman, with the only usual variation being the type used on the Cover Girls lamp in the case of Econolite and the type used on the Peacock lamp (and a few others) in the case of Goodman.

Leveling

This factor should be obvious, but we have spent hours leveling lamps on uneven shelves at collectibles shows, so it isn't always that simple. Even a 10 degree tilt can stop a motion lamp with internal parts in close tolerance. Using felt pads is effective for leveling legs or bases. Putting in shims will often do a fine job.

Moving, Placing, and Shipping

Hold a lamp with both hands when moving from one location at home to another. Fragile tops can fall off and break, shades can easily tip off and crack. Never move a hot lamp as a cylinder may touch a hot light bulb and instantly develop burn spots. Best to make certain that the bulb is cool before attempting to move the lamp.

Placing lamps properly is important for their well-being. Direct sunlight will surely fade colors already affected by age. Placing near heat may cause distortion, and placing near hot or cold air flows will cause intermittent operation. One time we could not figure out why a Goodman Niagara Falls lamp would spin everywhere we placed it except the one place we wanted it, on a parlor organ. We finally notice that there was an air vent behind the organ that would channel air upward and start and stop the motion.

How a lamp is packaged for shipping is crucial. When new, they were far more flexible and less affected by stress. Years later, they must be handled with loving care. We have successfully shipped lamps to areas as remote as Australia, so we have learned from experience what to do and what not to do. Following the procedures we suggest will greatly decrease the chances of damage. We usually like to ship lamps just as they stand. First, do not remove carefully chosen light bulbs. Then lift the shade and wrap a paper towel between the cylinder and the inner sleeve and over the pivot point to prevent chafing. Place large pattern bubble wrap around the lamp and put it in a small box filled loosely with packing peanuts, making sure that the power cord is wrapped under the base so that it cannot touch the shade and mark or dent it. Then place this sealed box in another larger box that will allow at least two or three inches of space all around the smaller box. Fill the space with packing peanuts which will cushion the precious contents of the smaller box from outside shock. Always wrap securely, but on the loose side so that outside pressure will not cause internal damage to an overstuffed box.

With glass and metal lamps, it is advisable to wrap the glass and metal parts in separate, smaller boxes to avoid interaction. UPS requires a box be able to sustain a several foot drop without damage. Often the drop off conveyer belts and the like is even greater, so you must do a thorough packing job if you want a valued lamp to arrive safely. Shipping by a faster method (Express Mail or 3 Day Select, for instance) will subject a package to less handling, so if the item warrants the extra cost, consider this alternative. Always insure the package for the full value needed to replace the item since many collectibles are not easily replaced. Remember that careful labeling and covering labels with clear tape will prevent loss or misdelivery. We ship many packages each week and even with the best packing, some damage will unfortunately occur. We hope damage does not occur to something on your top ten list that you have waited years to find.

Using Your Lamps

People often ask how long lamps can be left lighted. While we feel any collectible should be used sparingly to uphold its value, we also feel they should be enjoyed as much as possible. We have seen lamps left on for days that seem to be fine, so by all means turn on your lamps and enjoy them, but be sure to turn them off if you leave. Be more careful with the older ones, since frequent temperature changes may cause flaking on the inner parts.

❧ Restoration ❧

I now jokingly call my wife a plastic surgeon as she has skillfully "operated" on plastic (and all other) motion lamps. She repairs as many as six lamps a week for collectors and dealers and tackles all sorts of problems including cracks, dents, scene loss, and even the challenge of fabricating new cylinders and other parts made from scratch. Learning restoration skills may take years of practice and certainly takes some artistic talent. Following are the most common problems that can arise and tips as to what to do about them.

Warping of Scene Sleeves

This is one of the most commonly found lamp problems. Small dents, large dents, and rippled surfaces fall into this category. Reshaping using heat is the only cure, but it may be temporary (as described under warping previously). We encourage collectors to tolerate minor warping since attempts to correct this problem can lead to worse problems like cracking or buckling.

One problem is unique to Econolite. We call it "ring slip." As part of their construction process, Econolite used a glued cardboard ring to support the animation sleeve. This ring can slip down into the scene area with overheating or even excessive moisture loosening the adhesive. It can mar the scene surface with a ring-like mark all around and if it slips down further, it will block the light flow and the animation as well. Slitting open small areas between the bottom cardboard ring and the animation sleeve will permit a restorer to carefully force the ring back up with a ruler or a stick. Use care not to scratch the inner surface when attempting this. Either leave the slit open in case the ring slips down again, or close and re-glue with any white glue. You should not try this on a favorite or costly lamp.

This lamp is dented severely.

This lamp shows "ring slip" on the bottom third.

230

Scene Deterioration

This is the second most commonly found lamp problem. Scenes can become scratched, chipped, flaked, stained, wavered, or even partially removed. A skillful artist can touch up these problems, but a compromise has to be made between the look of the lamp lit and the look of the lamp off. What looks good when lit may look only fair when off and vice versa. Overall we feel touch-ups should favor the lit look, so leave the lamp on while working. Remember that unless you have skill in this area, leave the lamp as is, since a poor restoration will only further downgrade and devalue it.

This lamp has bad cracks.

Cracks

This is the third and most serious lamp problem since it may be most unsightly according to the severity of the crack. Hairline cracks can be easily glued. Small cracks can be filled and touched up. Large, gaping cracks can be repaired similarly but do not expect undetectable results. The greatest skill is needed to repair cracks and one must be willing to completely disassemble the lamp. We advise the novice not to attempt this kind of repair, or at least to practice on a common "junk" or parts lamp before tackling a valuable piece.

Never use any kind of adhesive tape to repair cracks. The tape will show and eventually yellow and harden, and will cause more damage when someone tries to remove it. Save your tape for shipping use!

Damaged or Missing Cylinders

As years pass, more cylinders will be damaged, lost, switched, or misplaced. It is amazing that often a lamp quite misshapen on the outside will have a perfect cylinder on the inside. Cylinders can be patched, glued, or even painted. My wife has actually recreated countless cylinders by copying perfect examples in our collection. The results have been great, often surpassing the limited effectiveness of old, yellowed, scratched cylinders. Using fresh, clear plastic allows light to pass through better. A fairly regular candidate for cylinder improvement is the Scene-in-Action Niagara Falls. Most cylinders in these lamps are faded with age. Restoring or putting in a re-created cylinder will bring the animation to life, pleasantly surprising the owner while not devaluing the lamp. Comparatively speaking, installing a replacement motor in a clock will not devalue it but will make the clock useful again.

Replacing Jewel Cups, Glass Bearings, and Fans

Jewel cups are not generally available, so one in need of replacement will probably have to be lifted from a "junk" cylinder. If a junk cylinder cannot be found, replacing with a small glass cup or bearing will yield excellent results. Glass is relatively friction free and will provide years of service. We have had glass bearings custom blown at a reasonable cost. They can easily be secured onto original fans with epoxy.

If original cardboard fins are damaged, thin cardboard fins can be attached. Metal fins are rarely defective. Using a sturdy mat board type of cardboard for cutting out fins will result in a perfectly suitable new fan for cylinders in need. You will have to cut fins that face either clockwise or counterclockwise or face up or down, depending on the direction the cylinder should travel. Test directional movement before permanently attaching the new fan.

Warped and Cracked Pleated Sleeves

Most Goodman pleated sleeves have held up pretty well. The plastic material they used is still white and somewhat flexible. We unfortunately cannot say the same for Econolite pleated sleeves. They used a type of parchment that has become brittle and has turned yellow. A recently opened factory-sealed Econolite Butterflies lamp revealed a near-white look that few pleated sleeves have today.

Warped and Cracked Pleated Sleeves continued:

With shrinkage and hardening of the pleats, inward warping usually occurs. This is critical because inward warping will jam cylinders. We recommend replacing badly deteriorated pleated material with new white translucent plastic. The plastic has to be carefully shaped and pleated, and sometimes you will find that fewer pleats will be necessary so that the finished piece fits properly inside the somewhat shrunken outer sleeve. The end results will look much brighter, clearer, and will be so much less frustrating than trying to get a cylinder to spin in a space that has become too tight. Similar to re-creating replacement cylinders, this procedure, when done properly, should not devalue an original lamp.

A badly warped pleated sleeve.

Damaged or Badly Warped Animation Sleeves

Animation sleeves (or glasses) are all-important and often neglected. Small holes that let extraneous light through can be patched. Worn or scratched areas can be touched up with paint. Minor warping may be heat treated, but severe curling or great loss of image must be corrected. This requires great skill and patience as these parts must be hand traced and stenciled onto new material. After that, realignment and proper fitting is essential. Fine workmanship will only follow much practice and your work will be hidden inside the lamp, making it difficult to distinguish from original parts. If the end result is fine looking animation, value should not be affected significantly. Anna once had to create a missing animation sleeve for a rare Econolite Eiffel Tower lamp. We had no original to compare so she created a sleeve from her imagination, using fountain patterns we had seen on similar lamps. The result was astonishing and the lamp performed wonderfully, to the owner's delight. We knew how close to perfection she had come when we finally saw a complete original of the same lamp one year later.

Dull or Aged Bases, Framework, and Shades

Plastic polish will work wonders on plastic bases and parts. Brass polish will bring out the shine on dull metal bases. If rust is advanced or plating is gone, don't expect too much except a smoother look. Dull finishes on older cast metal framework can be enhanced by first cleaning, polishing, and then coating with a simple household floor polish like Future. The result will be a much more pleasing look that will bring out highlights and detail in fancy metalwork and will far surpass the flat dry look it had before.

Do not attempt to use plastic polish on outer shades because you may remove part of the image. Clean only with a cloth dampened with some soap and water. Never use any ammonia or alcohol-based cleaners. Window cleaners, all-purpose kitchen cleaners and the like will cause images to run. Occasionally a very mild plastic polish will liven up the color images without removing them, but test unimportant areas first and then proceed cautiously. Never do this on Econolite lamps! The upper ring borders on plastic lamps often are dirty and yellow as are the cardboard tops. The borders will withstand polishing, but the cardboard tops have only a slim layer of paper (usually black) covering them and they are easily marred with cleaning and polishing.

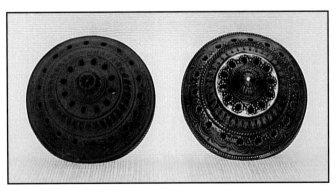

On the left is a metal lamp top as found. The top on the right has been restored.

The fan is a great trap for dirt. The blade may be crusted with greasy grime. Clean this area for smoother spinning operation. Also, always carefully clean cylinder walls and animation sleeve walls. Even a 60-watt bulb will be ineffective against animation patterns clogged with dirt and grime.

Don't forget to clean the bulb for the same reason. Think of a cloudy lens on a movie projector and imagine the same poor results on the proper projection that should take place inside your lamp. The reward for good cleaning will be evident when viewing your lamp afterwards.

Finally, it is our sincere request that dealers charging market prices clean motion lamps before offering them. Any used car salesman will agree that it is much easier to sell a clean, shiny car than a dirty, neglected one. If nothing else, think how a few minutes of attention will add to customer satisfaction and repeat business. Of course, if the dealer is not competent to clean without damage, he should just leave well enough alone. When pricing, a dealer should not put price stickers on shades or shade tops where adhesive might cause damage when a sticker is removed.

Fading

This lamp is faded.

Fading is a process that restoration can help very little or not at all. Red colors fade easiest and first. Bright reds can become orange or even pale yellow. Blues and greens are more stable and will usually only lighten in intensity and not change in hue. Without a doubt, color printing is somewhat imprecise and original colors did vary a bit. If over-all color is pleasing, satisfaction should follow without criticism. Judging color quality today may be challenging if a buyer has nothing with which to compare. Usually side by side placement is the only accurate method to compare the color of otherwise identical lamps. If you are lucky enough to be able to put two lamps together like this, the choice may be simple. Then again, it could be more confusing as one tries to decide which minor differences are better on lamps originally printed differently. If you must make a decision to purchase based on looking at just one questionable lamp in terms of color, then use the following guidelines. Colors should seem realistic and natural. They should be bright and rich, not muddy or dull. And they should be even. Often colors will be pastel since that tone was intended.

Many Econolite hand printed shades are pastel and are lovely in a special way. It seems that some of the color printing from the later 1950s and early 1960s is less stable than the earlier printing. The Econolite Historical Fires lamp tends to lose its bright red flames to orange or even brown flames. Of course, turning an Econolite lamp on will usually improve color from within, as noted in the chapter on their lamps.

Minor fading may be slightly improved by cleaning with a mild detergent. Or a gentle polish may dig deeper into the layer of better color just underneath the surface. Extreme care should be taken when attempting to improve color, as we have seen not only color but entire images disappear with heavy-handedness. Test a small insignificant area before proceeding. One collector has sprayed a clear lacquer coat on faded lamps to enhance the look. ("See, I can make Econolites shine just like Goodmans!") While this may look pleasing, we do not recommend this procedure. It alters originality and may cause more troubles in the future if the lacquer yellows or changes in any way. As with any older collectible, there is a certain appeal to having a patina. The perfectly natural effects of time will often add to the beauty and appeal of a lamp. We know of a collecting couple who recently opened a factory-sealed box with a 1930s lamp inside. It looked so stark and new to them that they put the lamp back in the box and keep it only for comparison to the identical, naturally aged one they proudly display.

Econolite Disease or "Econolitis"

This is not a special form of motion sickness. It is what can best be called a disease that may attack Econolite lamps. It is fortunately very rare and so far has only been seen on lamps by this company. The surface of a lamp that has this ailment will appear somewhat hazy in the earliest stage and then progress to having the graphic appear cloudy and even crackled.

The disease seems to occur with extreme humidity and moisture in the air such as when a lamp has little fresh air flow in a damp basement. We thought there was no cure for this disease once it started, but by sheer trial and error we discovered that heating the shade would cause an oily condition on the surface that could then be rubbed with a paper towel, eliminating the hazy look. Advanced stage cases may experience a much less successful cure rate. In any event, this is not a procedure for the novice since you may remove the scene and cause more problems than before.

Always try to keep your lamps in good environmental conditions, and at first sign of any problems, act quickly.

✤ Creating Your Own Motion Lamps ✤

My dear wife and co-author Anna was intrigued by the inner workings of motion lamps she took apart to restore. That curiosity led to her experiments with new lamp themes while the quest to find me unique gifts for special occasions ultimately drove her to make her own motion lamps. Some readers may want to follow in her footsteps which we outline in this brief section.

Using the pleated sleeve shade style that Goodman often employed is an easy way to start making your own motion lamps. A translucent plastic sheet can be folded to form pleats and then enveloped in a clear plastic outer shade that can be decorated or left plain. The real challenge is creating a plastic inner cylinder with graphics from your imagination or ones you copy from pictures.

You might want to be even simpler than that. Buy an attractive lamp shade with a likable graphic on it, remove the bulb clips, and add your own fan. The shade can then be suspended on a pivot rod attached to just about any standard table lamp. The direction the shade spins would depend on the graphic and your preference.

Of course you can go all the way and attempt to create a true animated lamp. Start with an image that interests you. Use old junk motion lamp parts or create your own. Badly deteriorated Scene-in-Action lamps are great for this purpose because the metal parts can be cleaned and restored while the glass can be scraped free of existing dilapidated old paper scenes. Aligning and designing the animation sleeve will be a challenge as this job was often done by engineers at lamp factories. You must mask off areas you do not want to show motion while creating patterns for areas where you do want to show motion. Use of different colors and densities will be important for the best effect. If animation sleeves are too dense, the lamp may look dark and dull. Finally, creating the cylinder and having it spin in the right direction at the right speed will either make or break a good lamp.

We encourage lamp artists to sign their work for future collectors. If creations are truly worthy, share them with others by producing copies or starting a side business. My wife has produced several worthy lamps you will see pictured in this section. I named them "Anna-Made-It" lamps to convey their function while at the same time using the name of their cre-

ator. One of her most popular lamps has been the custom snow scene. She creates cylinders and animation sleeves that look much like Econolite parts then uses a photo supplied by a client showing his or her house in the snow. The animation is snow falling on the scene. (See Penny Marshall lamp in Foreword.)

While animation has its limitations and some themes work better than others, this artistic realm has room for many new and creative ideas. We can tell you from experience the great excitement that comes from being given a unique lamp made especially for you. Close friends of ours recently gave birth to a darling baby girl and Anna created a motion lamp for them using a drawing of their home as the graphic for the rotating cylinder. She made the outer shade by drawing a stork carrying a baby bundle accompanied by Dumbo and other Disney characters flying overhead. When the lamp is lit and moving, the motion of the house gives the illusion that the characters are really flying in to deliver the baby! This remarkable lamp was a winsome combination of my idea and Anna's execution. It has become the centerpiece of our friends' nursery, giving us joy and pride each time we view it. There is only one problem here — I can't get my wife to make one for me!

Original Motion Lamp Creations

Anna-Made-It Icart "Yachting" (1994)

Waves churn by the vessel.

Made for husband Sam as a Christmas gift, this is a fascinating first effort by Anna. It uses a classic 1940 print by respected Art Deco artist Louis Icart. Anna took a standard Econolite base and a common cylinder and then designed the animation sleeve from scratch. Her work today is miles above this, but I love the piece for being a fine first attempt and a surprise that had me in tears after opening the package. Value: priceless.

Anna-Made-It Icart "Before Christmas" (1996)

Snow falls on the scene.

Made for husband Sam two years later than the above lamp. A cute Icart piece from 1922 was copied and then all inner parts were hand made to produce a picture frame style lamp. It looks great and works well. Value: Now that she is a pro at making these, she says it's worth about $250.00 in labor and parts

Anna-Made-It Gazebo (1995)

Dancers in black silhouette move around images of champagne glasses while the people look on.

Another custom-made Christmas gift for husband Sam. Using an inexpensive plastic bird feeder for the framework, she designed a Rev-o-lite type of lamp. It is special because family pictures fill the window openings. I suggested putting a musical movement into the top so that it would be one of the first musical motion lamps! Value: in the eye of the beholder.

Anna-Made-It Halloween Lamp (November 1995)

Cauldron bubbles, flames flicker, and outlines of figures glimmer while the pumpkin glows.

She made this just in time for Halloween. She used a store-bought wood frame lined with glass and a store-bought plastic graphic. All other parts were hand made, including the housing which looks like a giant Econolite picture frame lamp. Possibly the first animated Halloween lamp. Value: A well-kept secret since it took so long; she doesn't want to make any more!

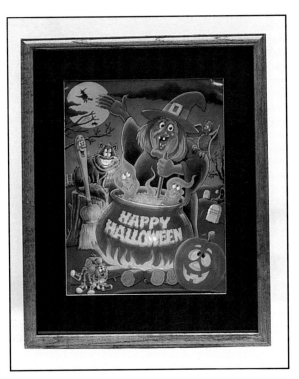

Anna-Made-It Snow Scene (1995)

Gentle snow falls on the scene.

This was made in honor of the Blizzard of 1995 which crippled much of the United States for long periods. Using an Econolite snow scene lamp and removing the outer shade, she attached her own graphic surrounded by a clear plastic sleeve. She has made a few custom snow scenes using all handmade parts for a few clients providing their own photos. Value: $300.00 for labor and materials.

236

Anna-Made-It Pink Flamingos (1994)

The birds rustle their feathers while water flows at their feet.

One of the best of her productions. She takes junk Scene-in-Action metal and glass parts and refinishes them. Using an authentic 1950s decal of pink flamingos in water for the scene, she applied it to the glass. All inner animation parts are designed and hand made. The lamp has been an instant hit with all who have seen it, and she has produced about eight signed copies to date. Value: $300.00.

Anna-Made-It Paul Miller Snow Scene (1996)

Snow falls on the scene.

Secretly using a photo that Paul's daughter Susie snapped while he was busy shoveling snow outside his home, Anna went to work. We presented the completed lamp to Paul as his Christmas present for 1996. His reaction was truly rewarding, and he now has it in a place of honor and considers it one of the top priority lamps in his wonderful collection. Value: It prompted me to request (and receive!) an exact copy for our own collection!

"Zorro Lamp" (1996)

The Zorro name and image spin by.

A lamp that is truly a hoot since it is made entirely of odd parts like a sink drain for the base, a sugar shaker glass for the sleeve, and more! Nick Maksymyk of Conshohocken, Pa., sent this to us as a gift to show what could be done with some imagination, skill, and little cost. It is really cute. Value: To inspire more work like this!

"Catharine's Lakeside Scene" (1993)

Water ripples and clouds shift.

Using an Econolite outer shell and animation sleeve, a Goodman cylinder, and a graphic from an old plastic lampshade, Catharine Fry made this lamp to add to her display of Goodman Birches type lamps. It is rich in color and fools you into thinking it is one from the Goodman series. Value: She and her husband Mahlon love it.

"Little Mermaid Lamp" (1996)

The shade spins around.

Paul Miller took a nice Disney Lamp and added a fan to the shade to turn it into a motion piece. It is quite simple but very pretty and effective. He presented it to Anna and me for Christmas of 1996. Value: Greatly improves a static $30 lamp.

"Paul's Snow Scenes" (1993)

Snow falls.

Using Econolite inner parts, Goodman bases, and plastic graphics he found on old lampshades, Paul Miller produced inviting lamps he displays with his other snow scenes, and many people have asked where they could find these! Value: If it looks mass produced and people want it, you know it has value!

"Deco Frame Snow Scene" (1930s, 1950s & 1990s)

Snow falls.

Dated to show a wide time expanse, this is another "marriage" lamp for which Paul Miller took parts from both Scene-in-Action and Econolite lamps and put them together. It is quite appealing as the vivid Econolite scene is nicely framed by the stately Scene-in-Action silver-colored body. It performs as nicely as it looks. Value: High at today's prices, since you have to sacrifice two valuable lamps. Try to use some junk parts!

✦ More Motion Sickness ✦

In an effort to show and tell everything we were aware of, we have added this bonus chapter as proof of our dedication to this work, the book we just could not seem to end. The following lamps are ones we and friends have found since our September 1997 publishing deadline. They cover many different categories and most were located in late 1997 and right into 1998. We felt that they were either too rare or too interesting to keep to ourselves, and fortunately for our readers, the folks at Collector Books agreed.

We would like to thank the following people for working up to the last minute to supply information and photos for this chapter: Lynn and Sandi Maack, Paul Miller and daughter Paula, Mike Myers, Russ Nicotra, Ken Paruti, Glenn Rossong, Lorne Shields, and Jim Whitaker.

"El Capitan Coffee" (1920s)

On the left, the walking Captain logo on coffee can changes color while below "No other coffee like it" flashes on and off. Scene to the right features burning fireplace and lake and cloud movement outside parlor window. Below that words in large letters change color from red to yellow to green.

Truly extraordinary advertising lamp produced by Scene-in-Action as a specialty unit. It features a handsome wood frame that is fancy and has blue borders with multiple colored accents. Inside, the rugged construction features two-tiered pivot assemblies each containing two bulbs for a total of six. This is the only lamp we have seen that uses three cylinders for the animation. Each cylinder is separated by metal dividers to keep light from interacting. (See detail photos on next page.) This very rare gem was found in its original wood shipping container which has the company name and address embossed on the lid and includes handles for ease in carrying the fairly heavy unit. Unlike most of the other large specialty units featured in the chapter on Scene-in-Action, this model was probably meant to be used as a counter display since it is fancier and has more subtle animation. When the lamp is working, the sum total of all the different motions going at one time makes this a wonderful piece created by a masterful company. A crossover collectible that might be even more valuable to coffee memorabilia collectors. $900.00 – 1,000.00.

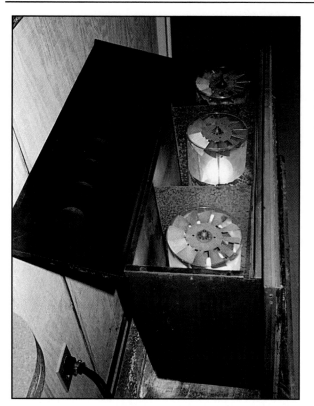

"Tee-Pee Lamp" (1930s)
Fire burns.

An unmarked lamp that has construction similarities to the Metal Fireplace series featured in the Other Lamp Manufacturers chapter. The cast metal framework is nicely detailed and the shape is unique. The fire scene is composed of heavy paper (instead of glass used in most lamps of this type) and the cylinder inside is the typical fire cylinder featured in all of the Metal Fireplace series lamps. The bulb is the same low wattage one used in the Ignition lamps and therein lies our basis for questioning whether this is an actual motion lamp or simply a neat figural lamp since no light shines through the dense paper scene that totally obstructs any animation. The back is missing on this example although we were told it should be heavy cardboard, which again would cast doubt as to whether it is a motion lamp since cardboard has no reflective capability. The temptation is to have my wife re-do the scene using a transparent material, but we have decided to wait until more information surfaces. Quite scarce. $250.00 – 300.00.

"Tivoli Gardens" (1950s?)

On front side fireworks burst in the sky at night, while tiny lights outlining the entrance to the famous park in Denmark chase like movie marquee lights. Also, various signs and windows are lit. On the rear, many fountains work, glowing yellow, while small border lights move.

Most likely a Danish lamp with construction similar to the Danish Forest Fire described in the European Lamp Producers chapter. The graphic is actually a grainy photograph of the sites. The outer shade has a shiny gloss and the scene is applied to its inner surface, like most Goodman lamps. The cylinder has a metal top and a vertical seam. Not all the motions are animated successfully, but this remains a nifty lamp, especially since it now becomes the second lamp we have seen to animate fireworks. Very scarce in U.S. $250.00 – 300.00.

Ginna Magic Lamps (1997)

Various cylinders spin around casting images.

Very similar to the Harmony Lamps in the Other Lamp Manufacturers chapter with additional wooden balls atop each corner. The sides are thin white plastic. With a 1997 copyright by Tarogo and a design attributed to Jim Gary, these are among the very latest lamps to hit the market. They are packaged in attractive boxes that picture every model offered except the Clown. There are nine different cylinders, Tropical Fish, Cow and Moon, Scenery, Santa Claus, Sweet Home, Ocean World, Dolphin and Whale, Space, and Clown. The graphics are richly drawn and colorful, making the projection superior to the Harmony Lamps. At a selling price of only $19.95, they are indeed a bargain. Expect these to sell for $50.00 and more when out of production.

Note: Another manufacturer named Elite Classics has just released nearly identical lamps with a few different cylinders, including Landscape and Cityscape.

"Six-Sided Ginna Magic Lamps" (1997)

Identical to the square lamps except for the shape and brown plastic corner posts. All nine cylinders are also available for these lamps. They cost $24.95. Again, expect them to rise quickly in value.

"Bulova Watch Christmas Tree Display" (1950s)

Tree revolves.

Sizable unit features a banner proclaiming "Give Bulova" in front of the Christmas tree. The revolving tree is made of plastic and in a store setting would have directed the observer's eyes to small metal racks that held the watches. $125.00 – 175.00.

"Sunny Brook Whiskey Display with Econolite Train Lamp" (1950s)

Train lamp operates.

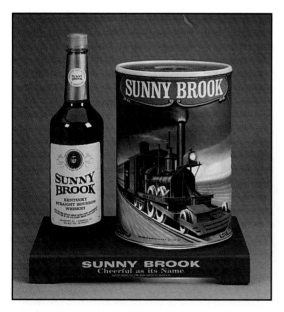

Using a standard oval Econolite lamp, the company added their own graphics and artwork skillfully to blend with the original design. The shade clips on the base bearing the product name and slogan "Cheerful as its Name." A bottle of the product (not original) sits on the left. We are not certain what the train has to do with the whiskey company unless the product was promoted for people on the go, but it is nevertheless a fine display piece. $225.00 – 250.00.

"Mirabella Gardens" (1950s?)
The fountains flow and water below ripples.

An unusual lamp featuring a silica front with wood bars on each side. The scene may be hand painted on the 12" wide unit that has an open back and a metal framework, with cloth braiding around the border of the bowed front. The lamp brings the Salzburg, Austria, attraction to life. Designed to be wall mounted or placed on a shelf. Very scarce. $200.00 – 250.00.

"Ko-Pak-Ta Toasted Peanuts with Animated Wording" (1930s)
Flames dance around graphic while words project through window opening.

Standing 3" taller than the standard Ko-Pak-Ta machine, this one seems about 20 percent larger. The framework is aluminum and the cylinder is positioned up front so that the words "Ko-Pak-Ta Toasted Nuts 10 cents" appear in the opening on the cauldron. With its sleek, sloping top, the unit is a stand-out. $400.00 – 450.00.

"Heaven and Earth" (1930s)
Color swirls radiate outward.

A mysterious and fascinating lamp as it appears that one woman is on earth and the woman above her is in heaven. Possibly attributed to Joseph Smith and the Mormon religion. It has construction similarities to Scene-in-Action with the large wood frame, glass and metal framework. It stands 23½" tall and is 14" wide. Inside are two huge cylinders that spin in opposite directions to produce the radiating movement. Unlike other Scene-in-Action specialty lamps, the scene appears to be printed on a skin-like material that is stretched as if over a drum. Quite scarce. $400.00 – 450.00.

"Merle Norman Cosmetics" (1960s?)

Cylinder revolves.

Using cardboard construction, the lamp stands 16¾" tall and is 18" wide. The graphic proclaims "new adventures in skin care" and the cylinder adds further information. Simple, but nicely shaped for counter use. $175.00 – 225.00.

"National Wood Frame Niagara Falls" (1930s)

Identical to the wooden Niagara Falls pictured in the National chapter except that the gold frame is smooth surfaced wood. $250.00 – 300.00.

"Fireplace Grate Motion Unit with Heater" (1930s?)

Similar to the fireplace units described in the Other Lamp Manufacturers chapter except between the two spinning fans there is a heater coil operated by a separate switch to provide heat as well as light. Made by Morris-Wheel Co., Inc. $150.00 – 175.00.

Illumy "Space Men" (1985)
Cylinder revolves.

This is the fifth known model of the Illumy lamp series described in the Other Lamp Manufacturers chapter. It features figural space men and rocket ship, and the cylinder inside shows men floating in space along with planets, stars, and a space station. A cute lamp that is hard to find. $100.00 – 140.00.

"Silhouette Airplane and Dirigible Lamp" (1930s?)
Aircraft fly over scene.

An unmarked lamp constructed uniquely since the two aircraft are made of brass and are held by brass arms that pivot around the bulb. When lit, the silhouettes of the aircraft are seen against the country scene. The scene is paper over a plastic form. Both the lid and base are brass. Extremely scarce. $275.00 – 325.00.

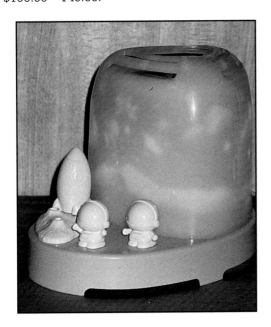

The following two European lamps are not shown; see story of their discovery at the bottom of page 128.

"Danish Antique Autos" (1950s)

Motion is very similar to the Econolite Antique Autos lamp, but the graphic features an old Opel on one side with a road sign that reads "Copenhagen 260," while the other side features an old Ford with a road sign that reads "400 Paris."

A nice discovery since it features cars not seen on any other lamp. Quite scarce in the U.S. $225.00 – 275.00.

"Little Mermaid" (1950s)

Waves splash onto famous Copenhagen statue while a boat in the background flashes its light on and off. On the rear side, the waves come to the shore while the lighthouse beacon flashes.

A Danish lamp that is quite appealing. The rear side curiously looks very much like the Econolite Lighthouses lamp with the perspective reversed. Quite scarce in the U.S. $250.00 – 300.00.

"Trav-ler Television" (1950s)
Cylinder with words and graphics revolves.

Neat advertising display piece for Trav-ler Television. The screen, screen surround, and control panel are one piece of molded plastic that is affixed to the heavy paperboard face of the unit. Scenes that project onto the "picture tube" include racing horses, a baseball pitcher, baseball stands and umpires, and an early airplane. The small screen below displays words like "terrific" and "built-in antenna." Most unusual. $275.00 – 350.00.

"Buddhist Prayer Lamp" (1933)
Colored circles project on the shade.

The plastic structure of this tall lamp holds a silk screen onto which the cylinder projects. Interesting shape. $50.00 – 75.00.

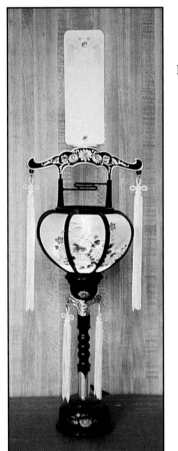

"Mushroom Lamp" (1960s)
Cylinder spins to create colored veins.

The white glass shade rests on the metal base to form a mushroom shape. When the cylinder turns, the illusion is that of veins seen on the underside of a mushroom. $60.00 – 75.00

Site Stimulator (1945) #S.S. 72-P
Cylinders project an inward moving vortex-like pattern effect.

Specialty lamp made by Econolite Corporation for a company known as Correctosite. The base, frame, front and lid are constructed of wood while the curved back is made of heavy paperboard. The graphic is silk screened onto glass. Two 9" cylinders spin in opposite directions in the upper compartment and are separated by a wooden partition. The scene below appears to be hand painted and no motion occurs in this section. According to the printed instructions on the back, the purpose of this unit is to "stimulate and exercise the inner muscles of the eye...has proved its value in scores of cases of defective sight...has been very beneficial for certain forms of nervousness and for use where relaxation is required." This is an interactive lamp, and the user must flip the remote switch to light the top half and then stare at the black dot in the center of the moving vortex for one minute. Then flip the switch again and the top half goes dark while the bottom half lights up. When the user looks at the scene, it appears to rush out to meet him and he feels drawn into it. The sensation lasts from several seconds up to about one minute with decreasing intensity. Call it swell, call it clever, or call it a quack device, but for the purpose of this book, we will gladly call it a rare Econolite specialty lamp! $300.00 – 375.00.

"Duquesne Silver Top Beer" (1950s?)
Top appears to whirl in colors.

Uses an extruded plastic mold shaped like a toy top and is framed by a paper graphic applied to a wooden structure. The words read "give it a whirl," which probably applied to the silver top of the product (probably cone-shaped) the user would open and then enjoy. Nice advertising piece with no manufacturer identified. $200.00 – 250.00.

"British Niagara Falls Lamp" (1950s?)

Water falls, churns, then flows downstream.

Very vivid motion is achieved in a simple lamp that is identified by "Laronde Lighting, London" on the base and says "Cascade Middle" on the animation sleeve. The motion is very similar to the fine motion of the National Niagara Falls lamps. Quite scarce in U.S. $175.00 – 225.00.

"Campari and Soda" (1960s?)

Two liquids pour, mix, and bubble.

On the left is a bottle of Campari liqueur, a thick and fruity drink. On the right is a bottle of Canada Dry club soda. The lamp advertises a nice drink made by mixing the two and it is vivid and colorful. $150.00 – 225.00.

"Christmas Tree" (1950s) #X-95
Tree spins around.

A slightly different version of the Goodman tree pictured earlier in the book. This features silver garlands and air openings only on the top half. Found in the original box, it also includes the gold foil top designed to form the peak of the tree, answering the mystery as to why several we had seen did not come to a point at the top! The original price was listed at $3.99. $150.00 – 200.00 with top.

"Christmas Tree – 15'" (1950s)
Trees spin around.

Two slightly different versions of the Econolite trees pictured earlier in the book. They differ with about half as many larger air openings. $125.00 – 150.00.

"Man and Woman Seated at Fireplace – Variation" (1930s)

Very similar to the lamp featured in the Other Lamp Manufacturers chapter except that the front framework is about half the thickness and there are no candlesticks on the mantle. Released in pewter as well as bronze finish. $125.00 – 150.00.

"Red Chinese Dragon Lamp" (1980s?)

Cylinder spins around.

Taller than average and somewhat fancier than others of this type, the cylinder features gods and goddesses flying in the heavens. Harder to find than smaller models. $50.00 – 75.00.

"Proscenium Arch Indian Lamp" (1930S)

Fire burns and water ripples.

The third known and rarest variation of the Proscenium Arch lamps described in the Other Lamp Manufacturers chapter and the only one of the Motion Electric Company lamps to use fire effects in addition to the usual water effects. Quite scarce. $250.00 – 300.00.

"Paul's Picture Frame Miss Liberty" (1958 and 1985)

Taking damaged parts from a round Miss Liberty Econo-lite, Paul Miller flattened out the scene and animation sleeve and placed them in a picture frame lamp. The result is a unique lamp that looks quite nice. The only part he had to hand make is the cylinder as the original would not fit into the small compartment. Value: Harder to judge today as the original lamps have gone up so much in value.

Twirling Shade Lamps (1997)

Shades spin above figural lamps.

As this book goes to press, this is the very latest release on the market. The two varieties feature the same shade (with toys and decorations pictured) that sits atop either a Santa Claus or a toy soldier. Quite nice and certain to become a collectible in the blink of an eye with values starting at $50.00.

We are ending this bonus chapter with what will be our very last gasps about lamps we know exist (and were unable to picture) and a lamp that is rumored to exist, and even two lamps that were falsely rumored to exist. Some we know exist include 1950s foreign lamp with naked lady standing before fireplace on one side and same lady in negligee on the other side; 1970s Taj Mahal lamp; 1960s Cole Swimsuits lamp with removable cylinder scene sleeves for variety; dairy advertising lamp with milk pouring. The lamp that is rumored to exist is a 1930s chalk lady with fan; light flickers on fan to give illusion of motion.

Best of all are the two lamps falsely rumored to exist, a very cruel blow for the seriously motion sick collector. We include them because they were rumored to exist for two years and word spread far and wide, but mostly we include them because they would be wonderful lamps if they did indeed exist. Ready? Imagine a lamp of the Fab Four, the Beatles with their famous mops blowing in the wind. And imagine an Econolite lamp of a snow skier coming down a mountain on one side and a snow lift operating on the other. The prankster who invented the idea of these should spend his time trying to actually produce them, rather than creating false desires in unsuspecting collectors. Fear not, fellow collectors, time has proven to us that there will always be more lamps to find, so let us spend our time dreaming about the unknown for that is what keeps the collecting spirit thriving.

Postscripts
or The Heat Goes On
Both Sides of the Story

We all know there are two sides to every story, right? But do we all know there are two sides to every motion lamp? Probably not, since all we can see facing us is one side at a time! A lamp can have even more than two sides. The scene may be divided by three windows like some pagoda-shaped Scene-in-Action lamps. Or the scene may have three different sections like the Econolite "Sailing Ships in Storm" featuring three historic vessels.

But the majority of lamps use a continuous scene that is divided into two sides just because of the physical arrangement necessary to shape a scene into the familiar round format. A seam divides the left side of the scene from the right and the two sides blend just like wallpaper seams in your home, thereby giving the impression of one continuous graphic. However, still only one side can be viewed at a time.

The point of the above is that you are left with a dilemma. How can you "look at your love from both sides now?" Obviously you cannot and must choose only one side to face outward. Lo and behold, many lamp companies have helped us with this dilemma in several ways. Some lamps have manufacturer and copyright information visible in fine print. The side bearing this information was intended to be the main or "A" side. This is the side the designer felt should be the front. Some lamps have actual titles or names printed within the graphic. Again the manufacturers have assisted us by pointing out the most important side.

When all is said and done, the choice is yours. Simply face your favorite side outward. We have listed suggestions below to further assist those who are still befuddled. We'll let you decide which of the following were written seriously.

1. Put mirrors behind your lamps to see both sides.
2. Turn your lamps around from time to time.
3. Buy more one-sided lamps.
4. Cover your least favorite side.
5. Choose the side with the most interesting animation.
6. Buy two of every lamp and face the different sides out.
7. Buy three of every lamp with multiple scenes.
8. Follow the wisdom of Solomon and cut your lamps in half.
9. Forget you read this whole silly section.

And here is a bit of trivia for the truly motion sick individual: Did you know that most Econolite lamps used black colored line cords, while most Goodman lamps used white colored cords? We "discovered" this while trying to hide cords in our photos.

253

Lamps Not Pictured and Lamps Rumored to Exist

In trying to present a book that is as up-to-date as possible, we have listed some lamps that were unavailable for photography. (The Econolite specialty lamps below appear in the original article included in the Econolite chapter, and a few other specialty lamps appear in the original article included in the Advertising Lamps chapter).

North American Trucking – Econolite specialty lamp

Kaiser Steel Blast Furnace – Econolite specialty lamp

Clayton Mfg. Co. Boiler – Econolite specialty lamp

Hatuey Beer – Econolite specialty lamp made for Cuban market

Gritt Advertising Salesman's sample lamp including Taxi cab ad, and other ads

Television set with advertising on screen

Motorola advertising – see Montgomery book

Wizard of Oz – see Montgomery book

Hudepohl Beer advertising – see Montgomery book

1964 New York World's Fair

Roto-Shade Nursery Lamp – see ad in Montgomery book

RCA Radio Batteries

International Harvester advertising – may be Econolite specialty Lamp

Nesbitt's orange soda – similar in style to small Genesee Beer lamp

Brew 102 Beer – same style as Genesee small table lamp.

GE yellow light bulbs – wild-looking bugs are repelled in a Plascolite Co. lamp

The following lamps have reportedly been seen by people at one time or another over the years. Those with a question mark are more unlikely to actually exist.

Atwater Kent radio advertising lamp

Sulky Horse Race

Submarine?

Indian in a canoe

Indian riding a horse

Cowboy and Indians?

Christ on the cross

San Francisco fire?

Scene-in-Action Snow Scene, Locomotive, Fountain of Youth, Wheat Field, and Canadian Mountie

Deer fight with antlers locked?

Bears feeding and fighting?

Diving horse

Baseball pitcher and hitter?

1930s-style floor lamp

It would be very exciting to see pictures of some of these that readers may discover. Do share your finds with us and we will be sure to share them with others.

Danish Snow Scene – swirling snow – action on shade featuring snowman, church, and cross country skier.

Grants 8 Scotch Whiskey – similar to advertising lamps with color blips.

Old Fitzgerald Whiskey – dots on shade glisten on lamp with pedestal base.

Ginna-type lamp – new release for European market with Eiffel Tower, Lady Liberty, and flying rabbits.

National Lamps:
"Lake Louise" – lake scene with mountains in background; "Two Ladies by Waterfall and Stream" – rare use of waterfall and stream in a lamp by this company; The Beacon Light – frame identical to Fisherman At Shore, with water and lighthouse motion, lighthouse is on left; "Lighthouse" – frame style similar to Jesus Christ on Water lamp, lighthouse is in center with water in foreground.

National Forest Fire – similar to round Scene-in-Action Forest Fire.

National Colonial Fountain #2 – the fountain scene in this looks like a beautiful oil painting.

National Gesso Wood Frame Sailing Ship – has wave action

Econolite Townsend Insurance Display lamp – large piece that pictures poor vs. financially stable elderly couple.

Michelob Beer – two plastic beer bottles at 45° angles with Michelob cylinder in center.

German Village Scene – shade simply spins around.

Drewry's Beer – highlighted images glisten.

Burger Beer – Ohio beer can replica spins.

Image lamps – new on the market, lamps similar in size to Tricycle lamps. Features three themes: Santa, Teddy Bears in Parachutes, and Flying Unicorns with butterflies.

Wanted: Dead or Alive

The words above could have been an ad placed by a small town sheriff long ago, but it would also serve as a new ad placed by collectors who want lamps in any condition. They want to find that one elusive piece and are often willing to settle for lesser condition until the day comes along that they will be lucky enough to upgrade. Condition is all-important for value, but not as important for collectibility. There are some extremely hard-to-find lamps you may never see again or wait many years to find, so why not purchase and enjoy lamps with lesser condition as a safeguard. We have always collected by this method and recommend it. There will always be a buyer for your cast-offs, as long as the condition is better than junk. Enjoy what you want now; waiting can be aggravating and life is all too short!

We thought it would be fun to list the 10 most wanted motion lamps in order of desirability by the most people. This grouping is based on want lists sent in from serious collectors around the country for the past seven years. We feel it accurately represents a good cross-section of the market.

1. Miss Liberty – What better lamp to be the most often requested on want lists than this all-American piece?
2. Venice Canal – Number two is anything but all-American, but is a real beauty nevertheless.
3. Waterski – The wonderful action is reason enough for high desirability.
4. Pot Bellied Stove – Unique design and stature puts this one up there.
5. Santa and the Reindeer – Rare and lovely so it is often requested.
6. Firefighters – Top quality action, wanted by all who see it.
7. Truck and Bus – Not really much better than the more common Antique Car but so much harder to find.
8. Moonlight – People often want things they can't find. This lamp is a good example of such desire, even though the readily available Japanese Twilight may be a nice substitute.
9. Airplanes – A real winner, so it's a shame it is not around as much as we would like it to be.
10. Serenader – With its classic appeal, it certainly deserves to be on this list.

It looks like Econolite is the leader with six out of 10, followed by Goodman and Scene-in-Action with two out of 10 each. If you already have all the lamps on the list, congratulations. If you have some, good show. If you have none, better start looking because the competition is great and steadily increasing. Lastly, if you don't want any of them, put down this book and start collecting something else!

Look to the Future

We recommend another collecting arena that will give you motion sickness. That rapidly developing disease is collecting electric animated novelty clocks or more simply called motion clocks. They all feature some sort of motion, usually light up, and as a bonus will tell you what time it is. Many people who collect motion lamps also collect these winsome clocks as there is an obvious similarity to their appeal. Some clocks use true animation while others use mechanical animation. Many even have rotating cylinders inside, but unlike motion lamps, the cylinders are driven by a motor instead of heat. Pictured below are two neat examples to whet your appetite. They are wonderful for bargain hunters as they are still frequently underpriced and will only go up in value as more people start collecting them. Hundreds of different and fascinating clocks can be found and enjoyed — but that is a story we will have to save for another book.

A 1950s United Lighthouse motion clock.

A 1950s Mastercrafters Swinging Bird motion clock.

Announcement

The authors welcome input from readers regarding this book and would like hearing about lamps not included in these pages. Even when we thought we had a fairly complete book, dozens of lamps came to our attention we had never seen before and we gladly added them to these pages. The hobby of collecting lamps will continue to be challenging and fresh since there always seem to be lamps with which you were unfamiliar just around the corner.

The authors are actively buying motion lamps and electric motion clocks for their collection and for re-sale. They will pay top dollar to get lamps they need. They offer complete restoration services and stock both original and newly fabricated parts for both lamps and clocks.

So, if you get the "motion notion," contact them by writing: Sam and Anna Samuelian, P. O. Box 504, Edgmont, Pa. 19028. Always remember to include your address and phone number. A self-addressed, stamped envelope must be included for a reply. Better yet, call them directly at (610) 566-7248 from 10 a.m. to 11 p.m. Eastern Standard Time on weekdays. Fax available during same times at (610) 566-7285. E-mail info@smsnoveltiques. com or by website at www.smsnoveltiques.com.

The authors' first and favorite lamp display rack.

❧ Bibliography ❧

Chance, C.H., "Motion In Advertising," *Point of Purchase Merchandising*, March, 1951. An interesting article written by the vice president of Econolite Corp. on customizing lamps for commercial clients.

Econolite Corp., *Scene-In-Action*, pamphlet from 1950s used to promote their commercial specialty lamps. Some construction details are provided in this glimpse into the inner workings of the company.

Montgomery, Linda and Bill, *Animated Motion Lamps*, L-W Books, 1991. Out-of-print pioneer work picturing about 110 lamps, prices, and some old ads and patent descriptions.

Various original company pamphlets, catalogue ads, articles, original instructions in boxes, and flyers. All of these provided insights into an area that has little documentation.

✤ About the Authors ✤

Sam Samuelian was born and raised in the suburbs of Philadelphia, by a mother and father who let him slowly but surely crowd their home with his ever-growing collections. Having sung in choirs since grade school, his love of music influenced his collecting. First 78 rpm records, then radios and phonographs, and later roll-operated musical instruments and music boxes captured all his spare time. He graduated from Temple University with a degree in communications (radio-TV-film). This led to his first job in the field at a motion picture film lab which spawned his collecting 16mm films of Hollywood musicals. After working in Temple's film library, he started a business based on film collectibles which began his career as an entrepreneur. An interest in collecting art led to another business, reproductions of the works of Deco artist Louis Icart, under the name SMS RECARTS.

Anna Arakelian Samuelian was born and raised in northern New Jersey by parents who were antiques dealers. Working in their store there and in Long Beach Island, N.J., she developed a vast knowledge of collectibles, learned restoration skills, and began collecting miniatures. After graduating from Kean College, she became an art teacher. Years later, she left to study law at Villanova University where she earned her degree. She started practicing law in Pennsylvania.

Anna and Sam met in December of 1988. By 1990 they were married and moved into their dream house. A few years later, they formed a business based on one of their strongest common bonds, collecting. They are happy to be working with things they collect, love working for themselves, and enjoy being a team day in and day out. Fascination with novelties nurtured their interest in motion lamps, electric motion clocks, transistor and novelty radios, and other specialized collectibles including figurines by Muriel Josef.

Motion lamps, being by nature so neat and fun to collect, became the top collecting priority and their shelves started overflowing with them, forming the base for the business. Anna's strong art and restoration backgrounds have been a prime factor in the success of their operation. Sam's mechanical and repair abilities, coupled with a keen sense for selecting and buying collectibles for investment and resale, have given them stability. Mail order is their business's prime focus while doing major collectibles shows like Atlantique City (N.J.) and the Triple Pier Expo (N.Y) under the SMS NOVELTIQUES banner adds fun and diversity. It is not unusual to see a display of 40-50 motion lamps and 30-40 motion clocks in their booth. Summer weekends are spent at the family antiques store on Long Beach Island, N.J., called The House of 7 Wonders, where quality general line antiques co-exist nicely with their novelties. When business is put aside, they pursue the interests that brought them together, namely dining out, going to the movies, antiquing, and especially public singing (Karaoke, anyone?). Although it is always a challenge keeping up with the demands of a vastly fluctuating economy, both Mr. and Mrs. S. know they have found their niche by dealing in very specialized collectibles. They love what they sell and like to instill excitement in others. The sharing of knowledge is a benefit to all. This book has been Sam and Anna's way of sharing some of their world with you.

❧ Index ❧

COLLECTOR BOOKS

Informing Today's Collector

For over two decades we have been keeping collectors informed on trends and values in all fields of antiques and collectibles.

DOLLS, FIGURES & TEDDY BEARS

4707	A Decade of **Barbie** Dolls & Collectibles, 1981–1991, Summers	$19.95
4631	**Barbie** Doll Boom, 1986–1995, Augustyniak	$18.95
2079	**Barbie** Doll Fashion, Volume I, Eames	$24.95
4846	**Barbie** Doll Fashion, Volume II, Eames	$24.95
3957	**Barbie** Exclusives, Rana	$18.95
4632	**Barbie** Exclusives, Book II, Rana	$18.95
4557	**Barbie**, The First 30 Years, Deutsch	$24.95
4847	**Barbie** Years, 1959–1995, 2nd Ed., Olds	$17.95
3310	**Black Dolls**, 1820–1991, Perkins	$17.95
3873	**Black Dolls**, Book II, Perkins	$17.95
3810	**Chatty Cathy Dolls**, Lewis	$15.95
1529	Collector's Encyclopedia of **Barbie** Dolls, DeWein	$19.95
4882	Collector's Encyclopedia of **Barbie** Doll Exclusives and More, Augustyniak	$19.95
2211	Collector's Encyclopedia of **Madame Alexander Dolls**, Smith	$24.95
4863	Collector's Encyclopedia of **Vogue Dolls**, Izen/Stover	$29.95
3967	Collector's Guide to **Trolls**, Peterson	$19.95
4571	**Liddle Kiddles**, Identification & Value Guide, Langford	$18.95
3826	Story of **Barbie**, Westenhouser	$19.95
1513	**Teddy Bears & Steiff** Animals, Mandel	$9.95
1817	**Teddy Bears & Steiff** Animals, 2nd Series, Mandel	$19.95
2084	**Teddy Bears, Annalee's & Steiff** Animals, 3rd Series, Mandel	$19.95
1808	Wonder of **Barbie**, Manos	$9.95
1430	World of **Barbie** Dolls, Manos	$9.95
4880	World of **Raggedy Ann** Collectibles, Avery	$24.95

TOYS, MARBLES & CHRISTMAS COLLECTIBLES

3427	**Advertising Character** Collectibles, Dotz	$17.95
2333	Antique & Collector's **Marbles**, 3rd Ed., Grist	$9.95
3827	Antique & Collector's **Toys**, 1870–1950, Longest	$24.95
3956	Baby Boomer **Games**, Identification & Value Guide, Polizzi	$24.95
4934	**Breyer Animal** Collector's Guide, Identification and Values, Browell	$19.95
3717	**Christmas** Collectibles, 2nd Edition, Whitmyer	$24.95
4976	**Christmas** Ornaments, Lights & Decorations, Johnson	$24.95
4737	**Christmas** Ornaments, Lights & Decorations, Vol. II, Johnson	$24.95
4739	**Christmas** Ornaments, Lights & Decorations, Vol. III, Johnson	$24.95
4649	Classic Plastic **Model Kits**, Polizzi	$24.95
4559	Collectible **Action Figures**, 2nd Ed., Manos	$17.95
3874	Collectible Coca-Cola Toy **Trucks**, deCourtivron	$24.95
2338	Collector's Encyclopedia of **Disneyana**, Longest, Stern	$24.95
4958	Collector's Guide to **Battery Toys**, Hultzman	$19.95
4639	Collector's Guide to **Diecast Toys & Scale Models**, Johnson	$19.95
4651	Collector's Guide to **Tinker Toys**, Strange	$18.95
4566	Collector's Guide to **Tootsietoys**, 2nd Ed., Richter	$19.95
4720	The Golden Age of **Automotive Toys**, 1925–1941, Hutchison/Johnson	$24.95
3436	Grist's Big Book of **Marbles**	$19.95
3970	Grist's Machine-Made & Contemporary **Marbles**, 2nd Ed.	$9.95
4723	**Matchbox** Toys, 1947 to 1996, 2nd Ed., Johnson	$18.95
4871	**McDonald's** Collectibles, Henriques/DuVall	$19.95
1540	**Modern Toys** 1930–1980, Baker	$19.95
3888	**Motorcycle** Toys, Antique & Contemporary, Gentry/Downs	$18.95
4953	Schroeder's Collectible **Toys**, Antique to Modern Price Guide, 4th Ed.	$17.95
1886	Stern's Guide to **Disney** Collectibles	$14.95
2139	Stern's Guide to **Disney** Collectibles, 2nd Series	$14.95
3975	Stern's Guide to **Disney** Collectibles, 3rd Series	$18.95
2028	**Toys**, Antique & Collectible, Longest	$14.95
3979	**Zany Characters** of the Ad World, Lamphier	$16.95

FURNITURE

1457	American **Oak** Furniture, McNerney	$9.95
3716	American **Oak** Furniture, Book II, McNerney	$12.95
1118	Antique **Oak** Furniture, Hill	$7.95
2271	Collector's Encyclopedia of **American** Furniture, Vol. II, Swedberg	$24.95
3720	Collector's Encyclopedia of **American** Furniture, Vol. III, Swedberg	$24.95
3878	Collector's Guide to **Oak** Furniture, George	$12.95
1755	Furniture of the **Depression Era**, Swedberg	$19.95
3906	**Heywood-Wakefield** Modern Furniture, Rouland	$18.95

1885	**Victorian** Furniture, Our American Heritage, McNerney	$9.95
3829	**Victorian** Furniture, Our American Heritage, Book II, McNerney	$9.95

JEWELRY, HATPINS, WATCHES & PURSES

1712	Antique & Collector's **Thimbles** & Accessories, Mathis	$19.95
1748	Antique **Purses**, Revised Second Ed., Holiner	$19.95
1278	Art Nouveau & Art Deco **Jewelry**, Baker	$9.95
4850	Collectible **Costume Jewelry**, Simonds	$24.95
3875	Collecting Antique **Stickpins**, Kerins	$16.95
3722	Collector's Ency. of **Compacts, Carryalls & Face Powder Boxes**, Mueller	$24.95
4854	Collector's Ency. of **Compacts, Carryalls & Face Powder Boxes**, Vol. II	$24.95
4940	**Costume Jewelry**, A Practical Handbook & Value Guide, Rezazadeh	$24.95
1716	Fifty Years of Collectible **Fashion Jewelry**, 1925–1975, Baker	$19.95
1424	**Hatpins** & Hatpin Holders, Baker	$9.95
4570	Ladies' **Compacts**, Gerson	$24.95
1181	100 Years of Collectible **Jewelry**, 1850–1950, Baker	$9.95
4729	**Sewing Tools** & Trinkets, Thompson	$24.95
2348	20th Century Fashionable Plastic **Jewelry**, Baker	$19.95
4878	Vintage & Contemporary **Purse Accessories**, Gerson	$24.95
3830	Vintage **Vanity Bags & Purses**, Gerson	$24.95

INDIANS, GUNS, KNIVES, TOOLS, PRIMITIVES

1868	Antique **Tools**, Our American Heritage, McNerney	$9.95
1426	**Arrowheads** & Projectile Points, Hothem	$7.95
4943	Field Guide to **Flint Arrowheads & Knives** of the North American Indian	$9.95
2279	**Indian Artifacts** of the Midwest, Hothem	$14.95
3885	**Indian Artifacts** of the Midwest, Book II, Hothem	$16.95
4870	**Indian Artifacts** of the Midwest, Book III, Hothem	$18.95
1964	**Indian Axes** & Related Stone Artifacts, Hothem	$14.95
2023	**Keen Kutter** Collectibles, Heuring	$14.95
4724	Modern **Guns**, Identification & Values, 11th Ed., Quertermous	$12.95
2164	**Primitives**, Our American Heritage, McNerney	$9.95
1759	**Primitives**, Our American Heritage, 2nd Series, McNerney	$14.95
4730	Standard **Knife** Collector's Guide, 3rd Ed., Ritchie & Stewart	$12.95

PAPER COLLECTIBLES & BOOKS

4633	**Big Little Books**, Jacobs	$18.95
4710	Collector's Guide to **Children's Books**, Jones	$18.95
1441	Collector's Guide to **Post Cards**, Wood	$9.95
2081	Guide to Collecting **Cookbooks**, Allen	$14.95
2080	Price Guide to **Cookbooks & Recipe Leaflets**, Dickinson	$9.95
3973	**Sheet Music** Reference & Price Guide, 2nd Ed., Pafik & Guiheen	$19.95
4654	**Victorian Trade Cards**, Historical Reference & Value Guide, Cheadle	$19.95
4733	**Whitman Juvenile Books**, Brown	$17.95

GLASSWARE

4561	Collectible **Drinking Glasses**, Chase & Kelly	$17.95
4642	Collectible **Glass Shoes**, Wheatley	$19.95
4937	Coll. **Glassware** from the 40s, 50s & 60s, 4th Ed., Florence	$29.95
1810	Collector's Encyclopedia of **American Art Glass**, Shuman	$29.95
4938	Collector's Encyclopedia of **Depression Glass**, 13th Ed., Florence	$19.95
1961	Collector's Encyclopedia of **Fry Glassware**, Fry Glass Society	$24.95
1664	Collector's Encyclopedia of **Heisey Glass**, 1925–1938, Bredehoft	$24.95
3905	Collector's Encyclopedia of **Milk Glass**, Newbound	$24.95
4936	Collector's Guide to **Candy Containers**, Dezso/Poirier	$19.95
4564	**Crackle Glass**, Weitman	$19.95
4941	**Crackle Glass**, Book II, Weitman	$19.95
2275	**Czechoslovakian Glass** and Collectibles, Barta/Rose	$16.95
4714	**Czechoslovakian Glass** and Collectibles, Book II, Barta/Rose	$16.95
4716	**Elegant Glassware** of the Depression Era, 7th Ed., Florence	$19.95
1380	Encylopedia of **Pattern Glass**, McClain	$12.95
3981	Ever's Standard **Cut Glass** Value Guide	$12.95
4659	**Fenton** Art Glass, 1907–1939, Whitmyer	$24.95
3725	**Fostoria**, Pressed, Blown & Hand Molded Shapes, Kerr	$24.95
4719	**Fostoria**, Etched, Carved & Cut Designs, Vol. II, Kerr	$24.95
3883	**Fostoria Stemware**, The Crystal for America, Long & Seate	$24.95
4644	**Imperial Carnival Glass**, Burns	$18.95
3886	**Kitchen Glassware** of the Depression Years, 5th Ed., Florence	$19.95

COLLECTOR BOOKS
Informing Today's Collector

4725	Pocket Guide to **Depression Glass**, 10th Ed., Florence	$9.95
5035	Standard Encyclopedia of **Carnival Glass**, 6th Ed., Edwards/Carwile	$24.95
5036	Standard **Carnival Glass** Price Guide, 11th Ed., Edwards/Carwile	$9.95
4875	Standard Encyclopedia of **Opalescent Glass**, 2nd ed., Edwards	$19.95
4731	**Stemware Identification**, Featuring Cordials with Values, Florence	$24.95
3326	**Very Rare Glassware** of the Depression Years, 3rd Series, Florence	$24.95
4732	**Very Rare Glassware** of the Depression Years, 5th Series, Florence	$24.95
4656	**Westmoreland Glass**, Wilson	$24.95

POTTERY

4927	**ABC Plates & Mugs**, Lindsay	$24.95
4929	**American Art Pottery**, Sigafoose	$24.95
4630	**American Limoges**, Limoges	$24.95
1312	**Blue & White Stoneware**, McNerney	$9.95
1958	So. Potteries **Blue Ridge Dinnerware**, 3rd Ed., Newbound	$14.95
1959	**Blue Willow**, 2nd Ed., Gaston	$14.95
4848	Ceramic **Coin Banks**, Stoddard	$19.95
4851	Collectible **Cups & Saucers**, Harran	$18.95
4709	Collectible **Kay Finch**, Biography, Identification & Values, Martinez/Frick	$18.95
1373	Collector's Encyclopedia of **American Dinnerware**, Cunningham	$24.95
4931	Collector's Encyclopedia of **Bauer Pottery**, Chipman	$24.95
3815	Collector's Encyclopedia of **Blue Ridge Dinnerware**, Newbound	$19.95
4932	Collector's Encyclopedia of **Blue Ridge Dinnerware**, Vol. II, Newbound	$24.95
4658	Collector's Encyclopedia of **Brush-McCoy Pottery**, Huxford	$24.95
2272	Collector's Encyclopedia of **California Pottery**, Chipman	$24.95
3811	Collector's Encyclopedia of **Colorado Pottery**, Carlton	$24.95
2133	Collector's Encyclopedia of **Cookie Jars**, Roerig	$24.95
3723	Collector's Encyclopedia of **Cookie Jars**, Book II, Roerig	$24.95
4939	Collector's Encyclopedia of **Cookie Jars**, Book III, Roerig	$24.95
4638	Collector's Encyclopedia of **Dakota Potteries**, Dommel	$24.95
5040	Collector's Encyclopedia of **Fiesta**, 8th Ed., Huxford	$19.95
4718	Collector's Encyclopedia of **Figural Planters & Vases**, Newbound	$19.95
3961	Collector's Encyclopedia of **Early Noritake**, Alden	$24.95
1439	Collector's Encyclopedia of **Flow Blue China**, Gaston	$19.95
3812	Collector's Encyclopedia of **Flow Blue China**, 2nd Ed., Gaston	$24.95
3813	Collector's Encyclopedia of **Hall China**, 2nd Ed., Whitmyer	$24.95
3431	Collector's Encyclopedia of **Homer Laughlin China**, Jasper	$24.95
1276	Collector's Encyclopedia of **Hull Pottery**, Roberts	$19.95
3962	Collector's Encyclopedia of **Lefton China**, DeLozier	$19.95
4855	Collector's Encyclopedia of **Lefton China**, Book II, DeLozier	$19.95
2210	Collector's Encyclopedia of **Limoges Porcelain**, 2nd Ed., Gaston	$24.95
2334	Collector's Encyclopedia of **Majolica Pottery**, Katz-Marks	$19.95
1358	Collector's Encyclopedia of **McCoy Pottery**, Huxford	$19.95
3963	Collector's Encyclopedia of **Metlox Potteries**, Gibbs Jr.	$24.95
3837	Collector's Encyclopedia of **Nippon Porcelain**, Van Patten	$24.95
2089	Collector's Ency. of **Nippon Porcelain**, 2nd Series, Van Patten	$24.95
1665	Collector's Ency. of **Nippon Porcelain**, 3rd Series, Van Patten	$24.95
4712	Collector's Ency. of **Nippon Porcelain**, 4th Series, Van Patten	$24.95
1447	Collector's Encyclopedia of **Noritake**, Van Patten	$19.95
3432	Collector's Encyclopedia of **Noritake**, 2nd Series, Van Patten	$24.95
1037	Collector's Encyclopedia of **Occupied Japan**, 1st Series, Florence	$14.95
1038	Collector's Encyclopedia of **Occupied Japan**, 2nd Series, Florence	$14.95
2088	Collector's Encyclopedia of **Occupied Japan**, 3rd Series, Florence	$14.95
2019	Collector's Encyclopedia of **Occupied Japan**, 4th Series, Florence	$14.95
2335	Collector's Encyclopedia of **Occupied Japan**, 5th Series, Florence	$14.95
4951	Collector's Encyclopedia of **Old Ivory China**, Hillman	$24.95
3964	Collector's Encyclopedia of **Pickard China**, Reed	$24.95
3877	Collector's Encyclopedia of **R.S. Prussia**, 4th Series, Gaston	$24.95
1034	Collector's Encyclopedia of **Roseville Pottery**, Huxford	$19.95
1035	Collector's Encyclopedia of **Roseville Pottery**, 2nd Ed., Huxford	$19.95
4856	Collector's Encyclopedia of **Russel Wright**, 2nd Ed., Kerr	$24.95
4713	Collector's Encyclopedia of **Salt Glaze Stoneware**, Taylor/Lowrance	$24.95
3314	Collector's Encyclopedia of **Van Briggle** Art Pottery, Sasicki	$24.95
4563	Collector's Encyclopedia of **Wall Pockets**, Newbound	$19.95
2111	Collector's Encyclopedia of **Weller Pottery**, Huxford	$29.95
3876	Collector's Guide to **Lu-Ray Pastels**, Meehan	$18.95
3814	Collector's Guide to **Made in Japan** Ceramics, White	$18.95
4646	Collector's Guide to **Made in Japan** Ceramics, Book II, White	$18.95
4565	Collector's Guide to **Rockingham**, The Enduring Ware, Brewer	$14.95
2339	Collector's Guide to **Shawnee Pottery**, Vanderbilt	$19.95
1425	**Cookie Jars**, Westfall	$9.95

3440	**Cookie Jars**, Book II, Westfall	$19.95
4924	Figural & Novelty **Salt & Pepper Shakers**, 2nd Series, Davern	$24.95
2379	Lehner's Ency. of **U.S. Marks** on Pottery, Porcelain & China	$24.95
4722	**McCoy Pottery**, Collector's Reference & Value Guide, Hanson/Nissen	$19.95
3825	**Purinton Pottery**, Morris	$24.95
4726	**Red Wing Art Pottery**, 1920s–1960s, Dollen	$19.95
1670	**Red Wing Collectibles**, DePasquale	$9.95
1440	**Red Wing Stoneware**, DePasquale	$9.95
1632	**Salt & Pepper Shakers**, Guarnaccia	$9.95
5091	**Salt & Pepper Shakers** II, Guarnaccia	$18.95
2220	**Salt & Pepper Shakers** III, Guarnaccia	$14.95
3443	**Salt & Pepper Shakers** IV, Guarnaccia	$18.95
3738	**Shawnee Pottery**, Mangus	$24.95
4629	Turn of the Century **American Dinnerware**, 1880s–1920s, Jasper	$24.95
4572	**Wall Pockets** of the Past, Perkins	$17.95
3327	**Watt Pottery** – Identification & Value Guide, Morris	$19.95

OTHER COLLECTIBLES

4704	Antique & Collectible **Buttons**, Wisniewski	$19.95
2269	Antique **Brass & Copper** Collectibles, Gaston	$16.95
1880	Antique **Iron**, McNerney	$9.95
3872	Antique **Tins**, Dodge	$24.95
4845	Antique **Typewriters & Office Collectibles**, Rehr	$19.95
1714	**Black** Collectibles, Gibbs	$19.95
1128	**Bottle** Pricing Guide, 3rd Ed., Cleveland	$7.95
4636	**Celluloid Collectibles**, Dunn	$14.95
3718	Collectible **Aluminum**, Grist	$16.95
3445	Collectible **Cats**, An Identification & Value Guide, Fyke	$18.95
4560	Collectible **Cats**, An Identification & Value Guide, Book II, Fyke	$19.95
4852	Collectible **Compact Disc** Price Guide 2, Cooper	$17.95
2018	Collector's Encyclopedia of **Granite Ware**, Greguire	$24.95
3430	Collector's Encyclopedia of **Granite Ware**, Book 2, Greguire	$24.95
4705	Collector's Guide to **Antique Radios**, 4th Ed., Bunis	$18.95
3880	Collector's Guide to **Cigarette Lighters**, Flanagan	$17.95
4637	Collector's Guide to **Cigarette Lighers**, Book II, Flanagan	$17.95
4942	Collector's Guide to **Don Winton Designs**, Ellis	$19.95
3966	Collector's Guide to **Inkwells**, Identification & Values, Badders	$18.95
4947	Collector's Guide to **Inkwells**, Book II, Badders	$19.95
4948	Collector's Guide to **Letter Openers**, Grist	$19.95
4862	Collector's Guide to **Toasters** & Accessories, Greguire	$19.95
4652	Collector's Guide to **Transistor Radios**, 2nd Ed., Bunis	$16.95
4653	Collector's Guide to **TV Memorabilia**, 1960s–1970s, Davis/Morgan	$24.95
4864	Collector's Guide to **Wallace Nutting Pictures**, Ivankovich	$18.95
1629	**Doorstops**, Identification & Values, Bertoia	$9.95
4567	Figural **Napkin Rings**, Gottschalk & Whitson	$18.95
4717	Figural **Nodders**, Includes Bobbin' Heads and Swayers, Irtz	$19.95
3968	**Fishing Lure** Collectibles, Murphy/Edmisten	$24.95
4867	**Flea Market Trader**, 11th Ed., Huxford	$9.95
4944	**Flue Covers**, Collector's Value Guide, Meckley	$12.95
4945	**G-Men and FBI Toys** and Collectibles, Whitworth	$18.95
5043	**Garage Sale & Flea Market Annual**, 6th Ed.	$19.95
3819	**General Store Collectibles**, Wilson	$24.95
4643	**Great American West** Collectibles, Wilson	$24.95
2215	Goldstein's **Coca-Cola** Collectibles	$16.95
3884	Huxford's Collectible **Advertising**, 2nd Ed.	$24.95
2216	**Kitchen Antiques**, 1790–1940, McNerney	$14.95
4950	The **Lone Ranger**, Collector's Reference & Value Guide, Felbinger	$18.95
2026	**Railroad** Collectibles, 4th Ed., Baker	$14.95
4949	**Schroeder's Antiques Price Guide**, 16th Ed., Huxford	$12.95
5007	**Silverplated Flatware**, Revised 4th Edition, Hagan	$18.95
1922	Standard **Old Bottle** Price Guide, Sellari	$14.95
4708	Summers' Guide to **Coca-Cola**	$19.95
4952	Summers' Pocket Guide to **Coca-Cola** Identifications	$9.95
3892	**Toy & Miniature Sewing Machines**, Thomas	$18.95
4876	**Toy & Miniature Sewing Machines**, Book II, Thomas	$24.95
3828	Value Guide to **Advertising Memorabilia**, Summers	$18.95
3977	Value Guide to **Gas Station** Memorabilia, Summers & Priddy	$24.95
4877	Vintage **Bar Ware**, Visakay	$24.95
4935	The **W.F. Cody Buffalo Bill** Collector's Guide with Values	$24.95
4879	**Wanted to Buy**, 6th Edition	$9.95